BREAKTHROUGH

BREAKTHROUGH

Fred Lemon
with Robin Stride

MARSHALLS

Marshalls Paperbacks
Marshall Morgan & Scott

1 Bath Street, London EC1V 9LB

First published by Marshall Morgan & Scott 1981
Reprinted
10 9 8 7 6 5 4 3 2

British Library CIP data
Lemon, Fred
Breakthrough. – (Marshalls paperbacks)
1. Christian life
I. Title II. Stride, Robin
248.4 BV4501.2

ISBN 0 557 00920 9

Photoset by Rowland Phototypesetting Ltd.,
Bury St Edmunds, Suffolk
Printed in Great Britain by
Hunt Barnard Printing Ltd., Aylesbury

When we give what we have
The Lord makes it enough.

Dedicated to John & Gertie Sams who have inspired me and to whom I owe so much in enabling me to understand more deeply the meaning of the Frances Ridley Havergal hymn:

Take my life, and let it be
consecrated, Lord, to Thee.

Contents

Foreword

As we trudged into Dartmoor Prison that cold winter morning to lead the Sunday service in Chapel, Fred and I stood under the forbidding greystone archway which announces in stark, moss-ridden carved lettering, 'Abandon hope all who enter'. But it was many years before, after passing under that same inscription to start his five years hard labour, that Fred Lemon had actually found new hope – his life had begun again with the unforgettable experience of meeting the Saviour in his cell.

After this remarkable conversion life both in and outside prison was very hard; he had to face severe tests and real battles from which his strong faith has been moulded. Supported by a loving and patient wife, Fred has known the strength of his Lord and the full value of intimacy in prayer so that his life today is rich in Godly experience.

Over the years, we have become particular friends, mainly through fellowship in the Christian Police Association, of which Fred is one of the more colourful and enthusiastic members. To write these few lines has given me a long-awaited opportunity to show my gratitude to him for the enrichment he has given to our lives.

I commend BREAKTHROUGH to you and your friends with the prayer that our God of hope may fill you with joy and peace in believing, and that by the power of the Holy Spirit you also will abound in hope.

Robin Oake

Preface

The risk of triggering off burglar alarms was one of the hazards I accepted when I lived by crime.

If I had set a bell off then I would have given myself one heck of a shock. Even if I got away with it safely I'd still feel hurt that I could make such a mistake.

With God's help I've been going straight for many years, but those old burglar alarms won't stop ringing.

I was going up north on a preaching tour not very long ago. While there I was due to stop with the local curate.

So when some of the neighbours heard that a criminal was going to be living in the area for a while, one said he would take the precaution of changing his locks, another took the keys out of his car and another said he would notify his insurance company as a safeguard – maybe all said in fun but no doubt indicating a real fear underneath.

It felt like a knife going into my stomach when the curate explained what had happened. I was surprised by the neighbours' alarm, and deeply hurt that people could be so mistaken about me despite the fact that I'd been going straight for over thirty years.

Battling onward through these times is no easy task. The Lord's work is not all sunshine, it's a tough fight too. We all have our battles in one way or another.

In this book you will read of many warriors. From con-men, coppers and murderers to businessmen, churchmen and soldiers, every one is involved in some kind of conflict.

And whether they like it or not, I believe they are all caught up in the biggest battle of all, a spiritual clash between God and his arch enemy the devil.

Some of the people in these pages chose to be on God's side. Others didn't. But whichever force you're with, I pray this book may give you helpful hints from my experiences to encourage you in the Christian faith and bring you a deeper knowledge of Jesus.

1: Rough and Straight

Young Jim could be violent but he'd always been friendly to me. So you can imagine how my heart jumped when he walked up to my shop one day and pulled out a gun. Let me tell you his story.

Doris and I get all sorts of people visiting us at work. Many of them drop in for a chat rather than to buy fruit and veg. Mostly they've read my other books, have heard me on tape or seen me preaching. They pop along to say a friendly hallo and sometimes want to talk to me about their troubles. You must be thinking I can't do much business if I get many of them like this but the incredible thing is that God seems to work it so we are not interrupted during these times. And customers just seem to buy that little bit extra later on to make up my takings. It's really great.

Anyway, it was a Friday afternoon in mid-summer and I'd just finished my lunch. This young fella, a smart looking sort with crew cut hair and an earing in his left ear, strolled in. He didn't look like he'd come for shopping.

'Are you Fred Lemon?' he asked.

I said 'Yea, that's right.'

'I read your book,' he told me.

Of course, straight away I was interested. It didn't take long to find out he'd been inside – an ex-con can always tell another in much the same way as he can smell a copper – and had wandered up to the shop straight from the courts.

I took Jim into the back room and he unrolled his story. How he'd get bored with life and take a car away for a joy ride. How sometimes he was innocent but the police had a go at him and tried to nail him. And how in his latest case he wasn't involved in any way but had got the book thrown at him.

It turned out he was 19, unemployed, and had ended up being fined £115. Of course he'd protested about it, saying he only got that each week on security and had to pay his mum digs money. But the magistrates had told him if he didn't pay within a certain time he would be arrested without a warrant and would go back to prison.

He had his haversack with him and was going to get out of Southampton and make his way to London. Although he was a leader of some of the boys, and they respected him, he'd had enough and wanted to get off out of it.

'You know Fred,' he said, 'Every time I'm in prison, or down in the cells, I speak to God and tell him if he got me off then I'd go straight. And sometimes God's got me off, I'm sure of it, but I haven't carried out my word. It's not that I don't mean it at the time, I really do, but when I come out it's the birds and the booze Fred. And then I'm back in the rut again. As long as I'm here I'll always get myself into trouble. So I'm going to push off and go back to London.'

I advised him against it. Those of you who have

read *Breakout* and *Going Straight* will know what life in the East End had done to me. Petty thieving led me to bigger jobs until I was a violent criminal, nearly a murderer on one occasion. I knew what the temptations could be when you are unemployed and I didn't want Jim to go the same way. Thankfully Jesus Christ actually appeared to me in my Dartmoor cell. I appealed to him for help and he forgave all the revolting evil things I had done. He gave me a wonderful new life. I knew he could help Jim too.

'If you really want to go straight I'll help you,' I said. His face lit up. But then with my next words it clouded over again. 'First though, if you're not going to pay the money, you just must go back and do your punishment. Come out, and then I'll help you.'

'Nar,' he said, 'I don't want to give myself up now. They'll only put me in the cage for the weekend. I don't want to spend the weekend there. I'll go off, sleep rough, and think it over.'

I didn't see him anymore for a few weeks. Then one day out of the blue he came into the shop again. It was to be the first of a number of regular visits.

'I did what you told me to Fred,' he said.

'Did you? Well that's marvellous,' I said, really chuffed.

'I've come back to ask you a few questions.'

'Right,' I said, laying down a sack of spuds, 'Fire away.'

Jim started off, wanting to know all sorts of things about the Bible and God. After our talk he said: 'You know, I've asked several people these things but their answers didn't ever do me any good. Yours are the only ones that make sense. I've been to ministers, vicars in clerical collars, I've even been down to one of the local churches. But it never did any good.'

How lost you can be in a church! He said a few people came up and spoke to him, some shook him politely by the hand. But that was that. A 'nice to see you' and then they went back to Sunday lunch, leaving a man hungry for teaching and fellowship. Not surprisingly, he soon got disillusioned with going to church, although he enjoyed the teaching despite finding some of it a bit too much to take in.

'What are you doing this weekend?' I asked.

'Oh nothing much, why?'

I had an idea. 'How about coming with me down to Bristol?'

So he came. That Sunday I was the main speaker at a meeting where sixty young people gave their hearts to the Lord. On the drive back I asked casually: 'Did you enjoy it?'

'Yea,' he said, 'all of them young folk coming forward at the end! It was an incredible sight. I enjoyed it.'

'Why didn't you join them?' I asked.

'No need to.'

'Why?'

'Well, I've already given my heart to the Lord.' Jim gave a big grin. It was the best start he could make to get his life straight. I was thrilled.

'Now you've got to move on,' I said, 'and first you should tell your mum and dad – and your mates.'

There was no doubt he told them because they all assumed he'd gone mad. The punk rocker boys in his gang thought he'd gone round the twist. Jim also insisted his girlfriend should read the Bible if she wanted to remain with him. She did. And gradually his friends began to respect him again. But it wasn't long before the devil started having a go.

'You know I'm skint don't you Fred,' he told me. 'Well, my mates have been after me. They want me to do a job with them. They've got a job lined up and there'll be three to five hundred quid cash from it!'

My heart began to fall as I looked Jim straight in the eyes. He could tell what I was thinking and smiled back. He went on, 'But I said "No! I don't want to know. I'm finished with that." Have I done right, Fred, do you think?'

'You done right mate. The Lord'll bless you for that.'

Next day my words proved to be true. I can see him now as he came through the door, a smile from ear to ear. 'Hey Fred! That Jesus guy! Great guy isn't he!' Jim gave the thumbs up.

I said, 'What is it Jim? What's happed now?'

'You remember me telling you yesterday my mates wanted me to go with them last night and I turned it down?'

'Yea. You did the right thing.'

'Not 'arf! They got caught Fred. And if I'd been with them I'd have got caught too and I'd be in the cells now! Jesus looked after me, didn't he?'

He was getting the message. I nodded. Then his face saddened and he said how sorry he was for his mates. There was real compassion for them and he was pretty upset. What was going through his mind I don't know but from then on I noticed a change in Jim. He wanted to go out and tell people about Jesus. Perhaps he was hoping that by doing this they'd make a decision which would keep them on the road away from jail.

Not long afterwards, while I was fixing my display of veg on the forecourt outside the shop, Jim arrived back and touched me on the shoulder. I was quite unprepared for what happened next.

'To let you know I mean business,' he exclaimed, 'Look!' From under his shirt he pulled out a .38 revolver. I was shocked and took two steps backwards.

'Cor dear, what are you doing with that?'

'You know I'm skint Fred,' he said, waving the gun at me. 'Quite honestly I could do with a few bob. But to let you know I'm wanting to go straight, I'm going to throw it in the river.'

'No, give it to me!' I demanded. 'A skindiver or fisherman is likely to bring it up.'

'No,' he insisted. 'I'll take it to pieces and throw it in different directions from the bridge. I could get a few quid for it, but I don't want it.'

Jim did as he'd said, and incredibly a few days later was on the way with me to the annual Christian convention at the Filey Butlins camp. I reckon all Christians ought to go there, it's a week of splendid spiritual food. To be taking Jim along was just wonderful.

The day came and we set off early. On the way I started telling him about some policemen friends of mine who were members of the Christian Police

Association. There was a time when I refused to believe coppers could possibly be Christians. I hated them all. Now I know I was wrong but Jim was like I used to be. He hated the police with real venom. As we spoke he told me how his resentment against coppers had built up from an early age. They'd put him away, he said, for what he hadn't done. There was no one he would love to hate more than coppers. I saw trouble ahead so decided to keep quiet.

It wasn't until we were nearly at Filey that I told Jim he was sharing a chalet with a policeman's son – he thought he was going to share a room with me. I broke the news that I was on the police team and we couldn't share a room for one simple reason. I was sleeping in the same room as a policeman. I wondered if he'd hit the roof, but he wasn't too bad about it. If he'd wanted to get out there and then, and start off back, he could have done. We were so near our destination, though, that he decided to give Filey a go and find out what it was all about.

The first person to meet us when we got out of the car was a big tough police inspector – in uniform.

'What's it feel like, Jim, shaking hands with coppers?' I asked later on.

'Oh, they've grabbed hold of my hands many times. But never like that!'

You could see he was apprehensive. A bit distrustful about these hated policemen all around him who apparently loved Jesus like he did himself. It took him two days to pull through. At the start he kept himself to himself. Of course he was sharing the chalet at night with this copper's eighteen-year-old son, but during the day he kept quiet and didn't really mix. All the time he was watching them. Weighing them up. Seeing how they lived. At meal times, too, he'd be looking at them as they ate, watching their behaviour, studying how they reacted to him. After forty-eight hours Jim spoke out. And this is what he confessed, not just to me, but to the whole table during one dinner time.

'I hated policemen. I've had one particular unfilled ambition in life. That's to murder any policeman I can – and get away with it. But now I can see that you lot here are Christians, the Lord has revealed this to me. And I want to apologise.'

I realised he wasn't laying it on thick about the murder bit either. That's why he'd had that gun.

By the time we returned from Filey, Jim was what you might call 'on fire' for God. He spent a week on the missionary ship *Doulos* when it pulled in at Southampton docks and was looking forward to what he now wanted to do most, go to Bible College to learn more about God and then move overseas to spread the word. While he was waiting to hear from the colleges he got a job with the council as a dustman. Things were looking up.

When things go well, though, that's the time Christians seem to get tested. Jim was. Soon he was off work through a bad back. It didn't get better and he had to pack the job in. Still, there were the colleges. But all the doors gradually closed in his face. The rigmarole of waiting was bad enough for him. To be turned down was something Jim hadn't bargained for. He wasn't affiliated to a church. That was the first problem. The colleges wanted some sort of sponsorship or church connection, which the lad had never had.

Jim started slipping back to square one but without the thieving. Why hadn't God answered his prayers? Why had God not allowed him to get into these places?

'I don't think I'm good enough for God,' he told me. 'I don't think he really has forgiven me after all. You keep saying he has Fred. But I've asked him in my prayers and he doesn't seem to answer.'

He was continuing his regular visits to the shop because he'd decided to apply for a Government training centre as a centre lathe turner and he wanted me to teach him maths. So he'd come in for lessons. I wouldn't say I'm good at figures but I've been in my business long enough to know my decimals and fractions. And that's what he'd been told to brush up on.

I started teaching him mathematics on my brown paper bags. He said he picked it up easily the way I taught him, though I don't know what was so special about it. Anyway within a short while, Jim was quite chuffed at his progress.

One day we had a little prayer and he then told me he still prayed by himself but only half-heartedly. He hadn't heard God speaking to him. I'm afraid this is where people frequently make mistakes. They hear in the books how God speaks to me, or how I speak to God, and they want to be like me. But they'd be right little lemons if they tried to copy! You've got to be yourself when you speak to God, not copy someone else. Often it's as if people expect God to talk to them verbally or they expect his answers to be painted in the sky.

I've never seen a message floating around in the clouds but it is not outside God's power, of course. He does in fact speak in a variety of ways to different people. Only once in my life so far have I known God speak verbally, and that was in my Dartmoor cell.

More often he talks through the words of the Bible. Millions of people down the ages have been spoken to in this way. That's why the Bible is sometimes known as God's word to man. God can speak to you even when you are not reading it.

A dear friend of mine, John Sams, once owed around £¼ million and was on the verge of bankruptcy. As he walked down the stairs he suddenly thought of a verse from scripture saying not to worry because it was going to be alright. He believed this was God's way of telling him not to be anxious but to trust for a remedy from the Lord. John did – and God honoured his promise.

I've found that God also speaks through people. They can give someone, even a stranger, a message they believe is from Jesus but which makes no sense to themselves. The receiver of the words however finds what has been said is relevant, helpful, and frequently comforting.

On other occasions I've noticed that Christians can be prompted to phone or write to somebody, and when they do they realise they have made contact at just the right moment to be of help. Once, for example, a Christian couple in Jersey wrote to say they had a big house and wanted us to come and stay for a free holiday.

I naturally wanted to go but felt I should wait and see what God had to say. I prayed about it and right out of the blue I received a letter containing £150 from a man I'd never met. What's more, he instructed me to have a holiday with it. To me, that was confirmation enough that God was speaking and he was saying: 'Go and have a rest Fred. I've fixed where you'll stay – and here's the money as well.'

I told Jim he had to regain his faith and have trust. He had to hang on to his beliefs and persevere reading the Bible.

When things don't seem to be going well it's easy to get fed up. But I soon realised there was a purpose in Jim's disillusion and I thanked God for it. What if they'd put him on the *Doulos* straight away, say for a month or two months? It might have been OK for a short while. A bit later, when he was out there in those far countries, getting no wage and working many long backbreaking hours doing menial tasks around the ship, would he have stood it then? How would his personality have coped? He might have slung it in – I don't know. The point was he was being tested. The tragedy was he couldn't see it. He wanted it his way. His way all the time. Wanted all the fruit immediately – before the seeds were fully watered and bathed in the rays of the sun.

Soon, Jim was blaming it all on God. 'If God is a God of love, how does he allow all the suffering?' A cynical expression came over him. He seemed to have forgotten so quickly what he was so joyous in accepting, that God showed his love by coming into the world so people would believe in him and find relief from their suffering.

Jim went back to boozing badly but God, I believe, was determined to show him once more his power. He wasn't going to let the lad go that easily! And as I know only too well, booze can make you really argumentative. God was able to show Jim his power over suffering of the most horrible kind – when you are at death's door with no Jesus beside you. He was able to demonstrate, in a strange way, that he had beaten death to give men life.

It wasn't Jim who nearly snuffed it, it was his younger brother, Mick. I'd already bumped into Mick on the pavement and given him a strong talking to. I explained to him how if he mucked about with the Lord and didn't make a decision for him, he'd go to hell when he died. That very same weekend the pair of them went out on the town and had a good few pints of Hampshire ale. They had a great booze up and at throwing out time they lurched outside and started skylarking around in the middle of the street. There they were, making out to have a fight, threatening one another with raised fists and daring one another to throw the first punch. They were so wrapped up in what they were doing they never saw the car . . .

Before they knew it there was a sickening thud and the motor had sped off into the night. Jim was alright, so were his mates, but Mick had been knocked flying like a human cannonball and was lying crumpled up a few yards away. He didn't make a sound. Jim moved over and knelt down beside his brother. A crowd had gathered round not knowing what to do. Someone said the boy looked dead. Jim thought he was too. From the light of the street lamps the blood looked an unusual colour as it slowly oozed from the lad's half open mouth. There was nothing for it but to try the kiss of life. Jim put his lips to his brother's but before he could blow air into Mick's lungs he had to suck the blood out. (Later he told me: 'When they said what I'd done I was sick just to think about it. It must have been God who gave me the strength to carry it through.') He started to shake Mick to get a bit of life into him and said, 'You know what old Fred was talking to you about. This is what it can come to. You're going to be alright. But if you'd have died you'd have gone to hell.'

What we didn't find out until Mick was well enough to sit up and talk in hospital was that during his unconsciousness he was in a private hell of his own, actually at the door of hell. He explained how, as he slipped away, there was this terrible fight going on. He was in a frightening place, he felt, and heard someone say: 'No! Not you! Not ready! You go back!' And of course he did come back to life.

At Mick's bedside I was able to talk to him once more of spiritual things. He had his foot and arm in plaster and had been in great pain. So bad, he said he wished he really had gone to hell – at least then he would be spared the physical agony he was going through. There wasn't time to continue our talk as a number of his young friends arrived. But he appreciated me coming. I said 'See you, I'll come again.' A few hours later Mick discharged himself. I haven't seen him since.

Jim thanked me for the little help I was able to give. He said he knew Mick was hard but he would continue talking to him about Christ.

That was the mysterious thing. Jim spoke to others about God, and he was a great witness to his skinhead friends. But he himself was running away. I feared he would return to crime. Deep down he knew what was right. He wanted to do God's will, yet at the same time he wanted the pleasures of the world. He was crying out to God but felt God was not there. But it was because he was mucking about with God and unwilling to be fully committed to him.

Enthusiasm can be a danger when people give their hearts to the Lord. It's like what Jesus said about the sower and the seed. The seed on stony ground doesn't last long. You're happy for a while, full of enthusiasm, but you dry up and wither away. Jim was like that. Choked among the thorns. The word of God was stifled with the cares of this world. He needed basic potting in the faith before he was ready to go out and take root in the spiritual desert. Jim was keen. He just wanted the rewards too fast.

I was going to end this story there, but I'm happy to say that shortly after I wrote it I had a phone call from Jim to say he had come back to Christ. And he definitely has. People were praying for him all over Britain and God allowed Jim to return to him.

Since then Jim has been out preaching with me and he tells how all the friends he used to know in borstal, detention or prison had vowed they wouldn't go back inside. They said: 'No more for me, I'll go straight this time.' But Jim says with one exception they are either back inside or haven't been caught yet for crimes committed since their release.

The exception is Jim. From experience he reckons now that if you are going to change completely there's only one person who can enable you to reform. And that's Christ.

2: Prison Progress

Prison gates are being opened all over Britain to let in the message of Jesus Christ. What a difference there is in Sunday services behind bars now compared to how it was when I was a con.

In those days we went through the C of E service book and when it got to the sermon part the vicar disappeared and the chief officer took a reading – not from the Bible but from the *News of the World* or the *Sunday People*: he announced the sports results from the Saturday, otherwise we'd never have heard them because we weren't allowed newspapers and there were no wirelesses. Prisoners could get hold of the local rags though, providing they had been there eighteen months and were 'on stage'. Now a prisoner can please himself whether he goes to church. Also, outsiders are now allowed in whereas in my day such a thing was never heard of.

When I was released I never dreamed I'd be going in and out of prisons for the rest of my life – but that's the way it has turned out. And I certainly never thought for one minute that I'd ever say I'd look forward to going into prison!

Many Sundays of the year you are likely to find me in prison – though hopefully you won't be in a position to! It's funny, but they were glad to see the back of me when I left them and now the authorities are giving me more invitations to return behind the walls than I can possibly cope with.

Don't get me wrong – I don't volunteer to go to prison services to have a cackle at the powers that be or to try and impress and win a following among the lads. The only reason I do it is to try and introduce people to Jesus Christ. He's the only person I want them to follow. I know it is he and he alone who can sort out the mess we all make of our lives, whether we are in prison or not. He alone can put us right with God. He did it for me and he's done it for hundreds of other prisoners. The least I can do is pass on what I see is good news to those who might not otherwise hear it. They don't have to listen if they don't want to.

Mind you, the authorities don't always welcome me with open arms. Sometimes they are nothing short of hostile. At one prison, the governor and chaplain were in favour of the meeting going ahead but it was cancelled two days before. It turned out that my planned visit had nearly caused a walkout among the warders. A union warder had approached the governor and threatened: 'If Fred Lemon comes to this prison and speaks to the lads then my fellas will go on strike.' The fact that the meeting was cancelled had nothing to do with Christianity because groups of Christians still go there regularly. It was just that the warders couldn't stand the idea of an ex-con coming back and being given a free hand to chat to the prisoners.

Another prison I planned to visit put the block on too. Then, when word got around on the grapevine about what had happened at various prisons I'd visited around Britain, they had a change of heart and asked me to go after all. Reluctantly, I haven't accepted their invitation. I'm not going to be used as a gimmick.

There was hostility too when I was up in Scotland one preaching tour but God got the victory there alright. What happened was that I visited the local drug addiction centre and spoke to addicts and alcoholics and a few who'd dried out. Some turned up later on that Saturday evening to a meeting I was taking and it was wonderful to see many people come to meet the Lord.

Next day, I took a singing group with me for my visit to the prison. There must have been ten of us altogether. As we waited to be met at the gates we worked out our programme for the service. When the chaplain and governor heard what we planned to do they told us we would have to cut it down. So I said: 'Alright then, I'll only rabbit on for fifteen to twenty minutes and the singers can cut out the trimmings and it will only be three quarters of an hour to sixty minutes in all.

'No,' insisted the governor. 'Forty minutes is too long. Make it half an hour.'

'Yes,' echoed the chaplain. 'Thirty minutes should do.'

I was beginning to feel a bit downhearted. The music group was starting to get the impression it wasn't wanted much either.

'How many will be there?' I asked.

'Perhaps a dozen,' replied the chaplain. 'Twenty

or thirty at most. They come voluntarily you know.'

I was disappointed because I'd driven a few hundred miles apparently to speak for just a short time to probably twelve men at the most. Still, I thought, if it's only half a dozen then it'll be worth taking.

Imagine our surprise when we got in the chapel to find it crammed full! At least a hundred were there. We had a great time, got on with the job, and the Lord blessed. I noticed the chaplain wasn't there for the ending. He'd had to go to another meeting, he said.

After it was over I could tell from the enthusiasm in the handshakes that some had been gripped by the message. 'Thank's a lot Fred,' one bloke told me as he made his way out and shook my arm, nearly wrenching it out of its socket. 'Glad you came, I could have listened to you for a long while.'

I looked at my watch and would you believe it I'd been speaking for one and a half hours! I never realised it was going on so long.

As we left, there was no comment from the officials, no thanks. They were like icebergs. But we'd come for the prisoners and the warmth of the reception they gave made us certain the trip was worthwhile.

The welcome I received at another jail, in the Midlands, couldn't have been different. The governor, a Christian man, escorted me to the gate and said: 'I reckon the message today has done the men more good than all the treatment we give to try and help.'

On that occasion I took a Christian police inspector with me and got him to identify himself in front of everybody. I always get police officers to do that. Sometimes it's the same copper who put a few of the lads in there! You'd be surprised how well accepted they are.

I tell the lads in my talk: 'No doubt you'd like to give him a bit of stick but my friend here is a Christian copper. There are many policemen and prison officers going to church. But that means nothing if they're not following Christ. Well, CPA coppers are, and though they may knock you off they are only doing their job. These blokes care, they don't see you all as real villains, they've got time for you. They're good coppers. I dunno what you think of the Bible but these fellas reckon it can help you and to prove they're sincere in their caring they put New Testaments in the cells and pay for them out of their own pockets. They're not bent. They won't manufacture evidence to get a conviction – and some have lost promotion because of it.'

From what I can see, God is raising up lots of Christians in the different professions involved in prison work and I believe they will be instrumental in a huge revival within our prisons. The revival has in part already started.

In one town I know of four Christian people in the police who are jailers. They never had a clue they would be when they joined the job as constables. Yet all four were appointed to the position of jailer. And what Christian policeman would refuse this kind of work, with its many opportunities to talk to different people about his faith in God? The people they meet are so often crying out for God – and they are finding him.

I was particularly encouraged during another visit to Scotland when I asked for a volunteer to read the lesson. A young chap came forward and read beautifully for us. It turned out he had become a Christian in prison. Later I learned he had murdered his wife on their honeymoon by pushing her over a cliff. Prior to that he'd had her insured for a quarter of a million pounds. Altogether we had seven lifers there in that prison and all had given their hearts to the Lord. The hymn we sang was 'Heaven came down and glory filled my soul'. I shall never forget it. Their faces just shone with joy.

On another occasion there was a lad in the cells at Portsmouth who had done a murder. A Christian policeman who was dealing with him got the opportunity to tell him about Jesus. Eventually the lad wanted to give his heart to Christ. There was no doubting his sincerity, for he told the policeman: 'I want Jesus, and I want him now, but I won't ask him just yet. I'll be sentenced to life very shortly and then I'll start my life sentence with the Lord. If I do it now and the judge gets to hear of it then he will think I have only done it to get in his good books and curry favour. So I'll keep quiet.'

There are similar stories in many prisons today, not just in Britain but worldwide. Inmates at another prison I've been to hold regular prayer meetings together. They include some very notorious lads. Word gets round when men converted in other prisons are being transferred and this particular group sends out a Christian letter of welcome.

People are frequently starving for the word of God and then want to experience what Jesus can give them. The last time I went to Dartmoor prison I spoke to about sixty prisoners. I told them how Jesus came to my cell; as I was speaking I could see the window of that very same room out of the corner of my eye. When I shook hands with them afterwards, I realised I'd started up a bit of a battle. Quite a number of them said: 'I'm going to put in with the governor and try and get that cell you were in, Fred.' They wanted Jesus to come back in there to them.

A lot of people want to see Jesus like I did, but I tell them that Jesus can come to them anywhere, anytime, if they're willing to receive him and truly repent. You don't have to actually see him in the flesh to know he is with you. When a girl or a fella rings me up and I rabbit with them I know I'm not imagining it. I know for certain I am speaking with them, and they with me – even if I can't see them. In very much the same way I believe if we lift up the receiver when we believe Jesus is giving us a call we will know he is there too.

3: Borstal Boys

Borstals and prisons . . . the end of the road for thousands and thousands of men and women today. But it needn't be a *dead* end. I see it as a junction with a choice of directions. The 'I'm-gonna-go-straight-from-now-on' road is a favourite, but when people get out and set off along it they don't get far. Only God can help them do that.

Happily, countless hundreds of people are finding true joy behind the bars of jail. Lives that have reached gutter level are being transformed in the cells, just as mine was. Not because the prison system is working but because God is working in the prison system. And that enables people to discover what real freedom, having your wrongdoings removed from God's record book, really is.

I feel greatly privileged to be allowed back into borstals and prisons, some of them the very ones where I served my time. Through these visits I am able to share my experiences of the Lord and let people know that the best guard of all for their life sentence here on earth is Jesus.

In Northamptonshire I had the pleasure of seeing twenty-four borstal boys giving their hearts to Christ. Some of them have since been baptised. After the service I'd asked those who wanted to surrender to God to stay behind; these two dozen lads did so as their 250 colleagues filed out from the borstal's church. They stood there in front of the governor, chief officer and some of the warders, so that everyone would know they weren't trying to pull the wool over our eyes. Then they took it in turns to come up to me, the chaplain and John Sams, my soloist. We asked their names, laid our hands on their heads, and prayed with them all individually.

I recognised the first chap who moved towards us. It was Andy, who I'd met a few months previously in another borstal where I'd been preaching. He'd got himself in some trouble and they'd transferred him. Since we last saw one another he'd lost an eye, but with one good eye he shed tears as he asked God's forgiveness and for Jesus to enter his life.

We were all choked at the response; it was incredibly moving to see these tough young lads, who were embarking on careers as professional criminals, get down on their knees and humble themselves before God.

The governor was impressed too and told me afterwards: 'I think this has done the lads more good than anything else.' The chief officer, who had watched the whole thing, confessed he was brought up in the Methodist doctrine but despite all his Biblical knowledge had turned his back on God. He believed in God but could not accept the claims of Christ. Yet he'd been so affected by witnessing the twenty-four lads come forward that he admitted, 'I would like to become different, to be a Christian and have the faith you've got Fred.' So the chaplain and I spoke to him and prayed for him as well.

There are many other instances of prisoners finding Christ, so many I could fill a book with them alone. But making a decision to go God's way is no easy way out, as nineteen-year-old Dan discovered when he talked to me after a service I took in a Merseyside borstal.

The governor and chaplain had specially requested me to go, and my friend the Rev. Ken Clapham made the arrangements and came with me. Publicity went on in advance and the governor said he had never seen so many boys in the church. There were over two hundred of them waiting to hear this strange old con who'd somehow got caught up in religion. I find it hard to keep my trap shut once I get going so I was relieved when they gave the whole service over to me. They cut out communion, just had a prayer and a hymn, then handed over to Ken who said a few words of introduction. He described what had happened to me and then started off a question and answer session.

'Now Fred,' he asked, 'what would you say your life is like now?'

'Right,' I said, avoiding the question, 'now before we do that I'll just have a little chat to Jesus.' I bowed my head and could hear the laughs from the audience. When I'd finished I told them the sort of thing I often tell lads in borstal services. 'Now then, I expect you think I'm a big con. I expect you've all got together and wondered what I'm up to. Some of you have probably read my books.

'Well, I'm gonna have a little rabbit to you, then afterwards if any of you want, I'll be prepared to talk to you personally and you'll be able to get it off yer chest and tell me if you think I'm making it up.

'It's not a religious meeting here you know. But don't make the mistake of thinking I've come to entertain you. I've come here to tell you what Christ can do because you're a load of mugs! Everyone of you. I bet you think you're clever, you go outside, you have a nice little "tickle" – and what do you do with it? You booze it up, you give it away, and then find if there's any left it gets swallowed up by the legal brief who's supposed to help you. But you still end up in here! And when you arrive, what happens? You want to get out.'

I looked around and saw nods of agreement. Their faces began to get attentive.

'You reckon you're tough. Real tough. That's great. But what about your mum, or your young pretty girlfriend? Some of you might have wives. Are they as tough as you? It's them that's suffering, isn't it?'

'You make promises, some of you think "Alright, it's dead easy in here. I'm not gonna change. I got caught this time but when I get out I'll be a better thief." So what's your ambition then? Want to end up in Dartmoor like me? Or is it going to be Strangeways, or over on the Isle of Wight? Is that where you want to go? What a waste!'

'The greatest challenge you can have is if you give your hearts to Christ. Money's not everything you know. You can't take it with you in here, or when you die.'

I went on to tell them about my books: 'Look, I

could get a few thousand pound from the sales but that's not what's important to me. I don't want it and I give it away. Many of you would probably say: "Cor Fred, give it to me, eh? I could really do with it! Give me a thousand pounds Fred and that'll set me up and then I'll go straight."

'But you wouldn't. You wouldn't go straight unless Christ was in your hearts. And no amount of money is going to get him there. The price of having God in your life has already been paid. Jesus paid with his own life when he came to show us the way back to God. But by being raised from the dead he showed us he was the key to eternal life. He can give you sufficient for all your needs. That's what I write in the front of my books when people want me to sign them – "Where God guides he provides".'

I looked back at Ken: 'Sorry, what was your question?' By this time I had everybody's attention.

I went on to tell them of my young life and how I could identify with many of them who came from broken homes and whose mums and dads were drunkards. But I added: 'There's one thing we don't have in common, that you couldn't identify with. Because I was put in the workhouse. I lived with the alcoholics, the drop-outs, the tramps, the vagabonds. I spent my childhood among them and they were very kind to me. But I had no love.

'From there I graduated from one approved school to another until I ended up in borstal. Then it was the Army and prison. I would have been topped if it wasn't for God. He showed me love. He loves you too, and he's reaching out so you can take it.'

'You may say: "Oh Fred, if only Jesus would do this to me. If only he'd actually show himself to me like he did to you. I would be like you then." But no, you wouldn't. That's not enough. Your heart's gotta be given to him.'

Dan had been taking all this in. At the end, many lads spoke to me but only he got permission to come up to the governor's office for a long natter. The governor asked: 'Do you want me to move out?'

'No, that's alright,' said Dan. 'I've got nothing to hide.'

Ken was over the other side of the room so the governor joined him and they began talking amongst themselves.

'What are you in here for?' I asked.

'I did a robbery.'

Our voices were just whispers. 'And what have you done with the money? Given it all away?'

'Nar . . .' Dan smiled and leaned towards me: 'I've got it stacked away somewhere. In a bank.'

He couldn't see the problem.

I said: 'You want to give your heart to Jesus eh? And you're then gonna go out of here and use that stolen money to help you go straight?'

Dan's face fell. It was going to be a challenge. A battle between a few hundred pounds and receiving Christ.

Like all boys in borstal he had a number of agonising decisions to make. We were unable to continue our conversation much longer but as I left I shook hands and said, 'I hope you do go straight when you get out. Make a go of it eh?' He nodded. I'd love to know what happened to that money.

In the governor's office I saw a big fat cat eating what looked like chicken. I said, 'Do you give him chicken?' and was then told it wasn't chicken, it was even better – pork. Leftovers from the Sunday dinner! (There were never leftovers when I was in borstal, and many times we went to sleep hungry and dreaming of feasts fit for kings.)

The governor then outlined the tragedy of the place: 'They get fed well and can earn a pound a week. But when they go outside again many find they can't get any shelter. Or the places they do get are not up to the standard they've become accustomed to in borstal. They find the grub is no good and they miss the comradeship. They know they are out on licence and they only have to get caught doing a crime and they will come straight back in again. So they'd rather be in here having a good meal and some company than being outside in the cold. We find boys coming back two or three times. They often intend to go straight but it doesn't always work out.'

I couldn't help reflecting on the governor's words as Ken and I drove off that afternoon. If only all those lads who've wanted to go straight would put their hands in the hands of Jesus, I thought, he would enable them to do it.

Sometimes I'm not able to tell the lads of the power of Jesus because they may have been disciplined and banned from seeing visitors. So I write to them.

Gerry is a lad in Scotland, a Christian, who corresponds with me regularly from his solitary confinement cell.

You've probably read some of the letters in the Bible from Paul, who wrote wonderfully encouraging words from prison himself. Well, Gerry's writings have encouraged me no end. Sometimes he would even preach to me! He found, like many before and since, how God can give you strength and a peace to pull you through severe hardships and difficulties.

Once he wrote to me: 'It's at times like these, in solitary confinement, that I really need the Lord and all the guidance and strength that he can give through his word and answers to my prayers. I actually blamed the Lord for my predicament and I'm ashamed to say I wanted to break away from it all. But then I realised that only I was to blame for my troubles and only he, my Lord and Saviour, could put things right again. I did all I could in the circumstances. I picked up my Bible and read and let it wash over me until I was comforted – after a few passages I was. It's great to know there's a source of strength and encouragement close at hand which everyone can find if only they will receive it.'

He was even able to joke about the governor asking him for my address so that I could be invited to go and speak there. Gerry told me: 'I hope you don't mind me telling him, only if I didn't I thought I wouldn't do my parole report much good.'

Another time, one Christmas, he sent me a card with best wishes for the new year. He told me one of the worst things about solitary confinement was that it prevented him attending the Bible class. (His mates thought he was putting on a religious act but he stuck to his guns when he came out of chokey, believing he could be used by God to encourage them with his answers.)

There he was, in the dungeons and looking forward to the new year, pointing out we should all be ready for when Jesus comes again. 'For it will be as the Bible tells us,' he wrote, 'Like a thief in the night!' He knew he had nearly two more years to complete but he was looking forward to the following twelve months 'which will be another round of tests, traps and temptations. On the other side of the coin we are reminded our reward is salvation and so I hope to make this a successful year, one in which I bring myself closer to Christ and pray for the success of others who wish to find his light.'

As I sat down at home to answer his letter a few evenings later, my mind wandered back to my time in prison and some of the occasions I'd been sent down to chokey. Soon all the bitterness, hatred and resentment I felt for some of them wardens welled up inside me. Thinking about the injustices done to me, made me really angry.

The door opened and Doris came in with a nice big cup of tea. Suddenly I was back in my own front room again.

'Oh, hallo love, what's the time?' I asked.

'Nearly nine,' she said. 'Have you finished that letter yet?' She noticed the blank sheet before me.

'Oh Fred,' she said, 'you've been in here nearly an hour now and haven't even started it!'

But my thinking had served a useful purpose, as I soon realised the devil had been having a great time.

He knew one of my weak spots and when he saw a chink in my armour, he was in in a flash lighting up those fires of hatred that Jesus has put out for me. I'd been reminded that Christians are always in a battle; one of the biggest problems in the church today is that people don't take enough notice of the devil. Their armour becomes pretty rusty and then they wonder why they're not living victorious lives – it's because the devil's got behind their armour (or the armour isn't there) and usually they don't even know he's there. (If you're not sure about the Christians armour have a look at Ephesians 6 verses 10-20.)

I thought again of Gerry. The devil would be trying to sow doubt in his mind and would be looking for the chink in his armour. So as I wrote back to him I was able to encourage him but also warn him of the ways Satan might attack. I said I could understand there was a fight going on, but God had not let go – and wouldn't. 'Gerry, you'll come out top if you hang on too,' I told him. And he did.

4: After Breakout

I cried with happiness when I visited a city in the north of England recently. There I met four ex-prisoners who were converted to Jesus through reading my book *Breakout* in prison. One of them was Simon, an ex-sailor and drunkard, who is now working for the city mission. It brought tears to my eyes to see the love of God oozing out of him. Just one look at him and I could detect he was an ex-con. It's a sort of sixth sense one gets, although if you've never been inside you'd probably fail to detect it. I am still able to recognise people who have been in prison, even after they become Christians. It's a useful method of making contacts!

It works both ways. Most people, after all, can tell I'm an ex-con – although it's pretty hard for them not to know what with all the publicity I've been getting. When I look at my photo, or see myself in the mirror, I can see an ex-con there. It sticks out a mile although I've been going straight for over thirty years. And that, I'm convinced, is due a good deal to the fact that God sent the right Christian people along at the right time to help me over the various hurdles. If any one of them had been the wrong type I would certainly have fallen somewhere along the line.

In the same way as ex-cons can recognise one

another, so can Christians. There's a wonderful affinity between them, a born again brotherhood. If Christ is in you then you can detect him in others. For when people are living to his standards then he can be seen in them and working in their lives.

Not all ex-cons are as fortunate as I and former prisoners like Simon were. People often ask me what happens to fellas like Gerry when they get out. Do they meet other Christians or are they left to fend for themselves? Fortunately there is a 'follow-up' and we endeavour to put people in contact with a local church group in the area where they are going to live. Sometimes they don't know where they will go so it's no easy task. We do our best though, and there are many reasons for tears of joy over ex-cons who have been led gently into the family of Christ and have grown in faith. Sadly, there are also cases where I feel like crying with anger.

What happens is that these lads get converted inside and when they go along to the churches they've been put in contact with the Christians there are very kind to them. Too kind for the fella's own good. The poor bloke has no chance to go off and get a job and start paying for his own keep because he is not given that opportunity. He's too busy preaching, if he's not careful. Often, all the churches want is to stick the ex-con up on every platform they can get their hands on and let him talk away to his heart's content about his life and how he was saved in prison, borstal or other penal establishment. The people lap it up and so does the ex-prisoner, who quickly adapts to the role he is expected to play. He is getting money on Social Security, people are bunging him a few bob here and there, and the lodgings and food are coming buckshee from well meaning Christians. But things can't last like this for long. After a while the affection wears off. There aren't that many platforms in the locality to go on, and the fella is in danger of drifting.

I maintain that a man has got to be tried over a period of time. When a fella comes out of prison I can quite see how tempting it is for his new church to want to show him off as a testimony to the power of God in people's lives. It's often exciting stuff, a marvellous change from the usual boring sermon. But the best way of showing love for a newly converted ex-con is to think of him first, not second. I would say to a church: 'Let him get a job, help him get a job, show your love to him in this way, but don't have him up on the platform for at least six months.' If the person proves himself over this period, and if it is the Lord's will he shares his experiences with everyone, then OK, give him all the facilities. It makes far more sense to do it like this in the long run.

Another trap can be a girlfriend. A sudden relationship with a new admirer can be disastrous for both parties in normal circumstances, let alone church situations when one of the people involved has just been released from jail. The snare is set when the girl, impressed at the wonderful job the bloke is doing for the Lord, starts associating with him. It might not be for romantic reasons even, it can be just because she wants to help him go straight. So she gets attached to him like a groupie does to a pop star, except without the sexual overtones.

Of course, it might be romantic involvement too. Given time, it can sort itself out. But rush any new Christian into something, whether he is just out of prison or not, and the results can be disastrous. I know people who got flung together on such a wave of enthusiasm for the Lord that they were seriously thinking of marriage in a fortnight – and there were many heartaches as a result. Just because a man and a woman are Christians it doesn't mean they are right for marriage. And if one of the parties is a supposedly reformed criminal then they and those around them need God's special blessing, plus the power of discernment.

I've known of lots of stories like my next one. I'll call the couple Heather and John. Heather had always been a good looking girl but she had never got married. She always said she was waiting for Mr Right. The years passed and she became heavily involved in Christian work, helping the down-and-outs.

There was so much to do and so little free time that there was never the opportunity to get out and meet the single fellas. Heather's life became her work and she came to the aid of scores of men and women in distress. When she reached forty, her friends decided that any opportunity there was to marry had long since passed. Virtually all the men she met were about as desirable as an old tramp covered from head to toe in manure.

Into this situation came John, a young, strong, handsome fella, and a Christian too. He'd just been released from prison for the umpteenth time. Before going back totally into the outside world he was visiting the unit where Heather worked in order to 'find his feet'. They didn't take a lot of notice of one another to start with, but Heather discovered he attended church regularly and she heard him openly witnessing to the other men about his new found faith in Christ. He quit smoking and began reading the Bible and praying. Her initial interest developed into a serious liking for John, and over the weeks they discovered they had much in common. Both were accustomed to having little or no private life and each shared a burning desire to serve God where they thought he wanted them. It soon became obvious to both of them that God wanted them together as husband and wife.

Married life was great. They were happy and the Christian work they did was prospering. For a number of years this went on until Heather became aware she hadn't seen John reading the Bible or praying recently. One Sunday he made an excuse not to come to church, saying he had a headache. Heather thought no more of it. Three weeks later he decided he'd have to work on that particular Sunday after all. Sometimes he'd accept preaching engagements. The Lord's work came first, he said. He missed more and more times of worship until Heather found herself going to church alone more often than she was with him. But as he continued to give his testimony in other fellowships, and by all accounts people were being blessed by his ministry to them, she didn't let it worry her too much.

What Heather didn't know until it was too late was

that John was a compulsive gambler, and always had been. He'd confessed so much to her, but never this secret. It came to light when John ran up very heavy debts and 'came clean'. Heather forgave him, they paid off the outstanding amounts of money, and got back to their job. But John's gambling hadn't stopped and he was running up even greater debts. He paid them by stealing. Not a penny of it came into the home. John must have conned scores of people out of large and small sums of cash, property too. He was robbing Peter to pay Paul.

When they had married Heather hadn't realised John was a gambler, let alone a compulsive one. She didn't look for, or recognise, the signs. By the time she could read the signs the situation was out of control.

I'm afraid John ended up in prison again, not once or twice but many times. Every time he was there he insisted he wanted Jesus' help. Yet when he was out he didn't want to know. Each occasion he was released meant the beginning of another catalogue of gambling and conning.

While he was doing this, Heather would be at home, praying for him as she did the housework, dreading every knock at the door in case it meant the start of another court case and maybe yet one more spell inside.

With all the time she had to herself there was the opportunity to think through her plight. She went over their whole relationship together in her mind and realised that John had most likely conned her all along too, as well as their friends. Heather doubted whether he ever had been converted. The emphasis of his preaching on the platforms had always been 'See! Look what I have become!' rather than 'See the one who brought me from the pit!'.

Heather prays for the Holy Spirit to renew John. She believes in time he will be healed from his gambling disease. But meanwhile she lives under the tremendous pressure of sharing the same home as a constantly law-breaking husband. I wonder what Heather would have heard if she had given more time for the Lord to speak to her when marriage to John seemed so right. Sadly, there's countless other men and women thinking the very same question about their own partners.

5: Soldier Ernie

I meet lots of soldiers in everyday life. Not so much blokes in the forces but ordinary people who find existence seems to be made up of a whole series of battles. No sooner have they got one fight out of the way than there's another looming out of the horizon. There seems to be no peace for them. Rather like a boxer in the ring at those old fairgrounds. As soon as he's defeated his opponent there's another fighter climbing through the ropes.

Perhaps you feel like that. You find there's never a chance to celebrate because as soon as you win one contest all life's problems are lining up ready to knock you flat on your back again. That's how it seemed to me. One endless battle with never a chance for a breather.

That's just how it was for my mate Ernie too, a real fighting soldier of a chap if ever there was one. Like me, Ernie was born in the East End, living in great poverty in the rough and tumble of back street city life. But unlike me he came into the world right slap bang in the middle of a full scale war.

Ernie 'arrived' in an air raid shelter during a bombing attack. His young mother and father had started their married life in Elm Park, reasonably trouble-free in peace time but not exactly the safest place for civilians to be during the war. For close by there was a fighter station and Ernie saw a lot of the young pilots, who were later to play such an important role in the Battle of Britain, involved in dog-fights over his home. As a lad he saw a lot of bombs too. His home suffered near misses a number of times and on three occasions the rescue services dug Ernie out from the shelter. His lessons in survival came at an early age.

After the war he started attending primary school and graduated from there to a crime college – the local secondary school. It was a real centre for education. Not so much a school to learn the traditional three R's that they tried so hard to drum into me, reading, writing and 'rithmetic, but somewhere to study the three F's – fighting, fieving and faking.

The place was riddled with crime. People said Ernie's school typified the problems of the East End. Girls moved up through the classes straight into women's prisons and boys graduated to prisons, borstals and training centres. The girls went in largely as the result of vice charges. For boys it was usually violence that got them put away. Many of them carried small arms like knives and sharp, curved cut-throat razors. They were so unruly that police often escorted them to school. Their victims could be anyone who happened to be in the way, other children, gangs, or a teacher. The masters didn't dare walk the streets until long after the children had gone home.

With no authority to control them the children were eventually not content with bashing one another or people known to them. They ruled a reign of terror over harmless and defenceless old age pensioners. Many old men and women were left bewildered, helpless and hurt on the pavement having been robbed of the few savings they had and thrown cruelly to the ground by the juvenile mobs.

Ernie was amazed when he was in school one day and a man he'd never seen before brought in a boxful of books. They were New Testaments. Books! These were going to be given out as presents! Ernie was very excited. Most of the books he remembered seeing were boring outdated school books. He'd never owned a brand new book in his life. And a present! Well . . . Ernie got to wondering what the stories in the book were about when the headmaster stood up to speak.

The classroom fell silent as the teacher boomed his usual fearful battle cry: 'You lot! You all came from the gutters! Your families came from the slums. You were born in the gutters. And that's where you'll live too. I'll tell you something else. You're all going to die in the gutters. You're filth – and Christianity isn't for the likes of you. It's for respectable people who go to church.' That was the way the headmaster introduced the visitor. He sat down. Then the man, looking rather taken aback, slowly rose to his feet to talk.

This time there was a calm voice. When he spoke the words were soft. He sounded friendly. Ernie and his chums weren't used to hearing grown-ups talk *to* them. Usually it was *at* them. This man was certainly different. He told the school he was from The

Gideons, a society who distribute Bibles free of charge to schoolchildren, guests in hotels and many other people who may not own a copy. The man's message was simple, but young Ernie still found it difficult to understand.

The Gideon said: 'God loves you. All of you. He let his son Jesus die for you. He is reaching out to you through his son Jesus. He wants you to reach out to him by taking a New Testament and reading it.'

Ernie had no hesitation in taking his copy. You rarely got anything buckshee in those days. After school he ran all the way home and showed the strange book to his mother. 'Look what I got given at school Mum. A man came from the Giddy people and gave a whole boxful of 'em away.'

But Ernie's mother could not see to read very well because she firmly refused to buy new glasses. She spent what little she could scrape together on her growing family. So Ernie read to her from teatime until the sun was setting and it got too dark in their tiny living room to see any more of the small print. Ernie had been reading about Jesus and his dealings with people, how he helped them and healed them. And it got him wondering.

Could Jesus do anything for his dad? No one seemed to know what his sickness was. Three doctors had seen him and they all pronounced different verdicts. One said he had sugar diabetes. Well, Ernie didn't know much about that but he knew his father had something else wrong too. The second physician thought it was some kind of devil possession. Doctor number three said the man was insane. Life in Ernie's home might be just like any other poor East Ender's except that every three or four weeks his father would suddenly rush up in a rage and attack the nearest person to him. Usually it was Ernie's mum.

What the doctors did agree on was that at times like these, the man had the strength of three. Little Ernie disagreed. He'd actually seen his father fight with six men. Only when the seventh arrived were they able to overpower him and hold him down. And that was quite something when you consider he weighed only seven stone and was knocking on death's door.

Ernie was determined that his father should be knocking on heaven's door when the time came. As he sat thinking about the stories he'd just read of Jesus he found he was smiling. He was feeling tremendously happy, a terrific joy seemed to be spreading all around him. It was as if it came from the words of scripture, perhaps this was what Jesus could make you feel like, he thought. Well then, surely Jesus could help his dad! After all, Jesus had brought Lazarus back to life after he'd been dead a few days!

Not long afterwards the initial flood of joy apparently left Ernie. He was twelve years old and quite big enough to take care of himself on the streets, but he didn't know what to do about his dad. He badly needed advice. But from where? In the short yet eventful life he'd never known anyone who had ever been to church unless it was for a wedding or funeral.

Ernie decided to trek off in search of a church. Eventually he found one and went inside. A man who said he was a sweet salesman got up to preach.

'You're going to heaven!' he thundered. Ernie felt chuffed. But the sentence wasn't over. 'Or you're going to hell!' Ernie felt a lump in his throat. The man started talking in the same way the Gideon had spoken. 'If you want to go to heaven, come to Jesus.' Ernie was gripping the pew where he sat with both hands. He bit his lip and looked around at all the men, women, boys and girls in their Sunday-best. He wanted to scarper. He tried to move but his legs were all weak. It seems to me it was God's way of making him stay put until he had decided one way or the other.

Ernie bowed his head, shut his eyes, and decided to come to Jesus. He went to say the words the man said he must say if he truly wanted to follow Jesus. Before he could say anything though, it was as if Jesus had come to him. A kind of healing took place deep inside. To Ernie it was like two busted bones linking together. A huge weight left Ernie's shoulders, and unaware that he should have told someone in the church what had happened, he went home immediately after the service. On the way it started to rain so he ran the last bit.

When he opened the back door his sister Jill was waiting there for him. Her face matched the sky outside. Grey. 'Dad's ill,' she told him. Ernie knew it was something really serious. He didn't find out until many years later that in church his decision to follow Jesus amounted to what Christians call a 'conversion', but he certainly felt different. And he felt confident.

'Where is he?'

'In the sitting room with Mum. Be careful Ernie.'

He walked through to find his father jabbing a bread knife at his mother's face. She was backing away and a few of the lunges were bringing the tip of the weapon into contact with her face. Ernie froze for a second, unable to fathom how she'd not already been stabbed. In her hand was a small bottle. She'd obviously been trying to get Dad to take his medicine when it triggered him off and he'd gone bonkers.

Father saw Ernie standing there and started shouting, daring him to take the knife off him: 'Come on then son, grab hold of it! Get it off me! Bet you couldn't! See if you dare!'

Ernie, fighting back tears, bravely strutted into the centre of the room and said the only prayer he knew. 'God help me!' Suddenly his dad stood stock still and threw the knife onto the carpet as if it was a white hot piece of metal. He burst into tears, collapsed into a chair, and sobbed for three days.

No one ever saw him ill like that again. Now then, you'd think all this would have made Ernie only too eager to continue in his new found faith in God, wouldn't you! But it didn't. He forgot all about his promise to follow Jesus – until his next big battle was ready for him.

Coming home from work one evening he saw his mother waiting for him at the front door. She had some disturbing news for him: 'I've got cancer,' she said. 'I think I'm dying; look after Dad and your sisters.' Then she added: 'Do you think I should go into hospital?' Ernie said he thought she should, so after going upstairs to pack she kissed the family goodbye, and set off.

Next day Ernie visited her but found it difficult to know what to say. He looked around the ward, trying to find the inspiration to put a sentence or two together. At the next bed he saw a young girl was visiting an old lady. On the blankets lay a Bible and the couple were laughing with joy. They had a peace and a happiness which Ernie wanted more than anything else in the world. Seeing them had reminded him of his promise five years earlier in that church where the sweet salesman was preaching. Ernie asked God to take him back.

As soon as he could he went back to the very same church and shared with the leaders there what had happened. They told him he had become a Christian, and asked if he would like to take communion and be baptised. Ernie said 'Yes'.

One of the first prayers he prayed after walking up the steps out of the baptismal pool, which was like a little swimming baths at the front of the church, was for his mother. It turned out that following an operation she was to have many more years of life.

To Ernie, adult baptism was what Jesus had and it was what Jesus wanted of his followers. So there wasn't anything all that odd about it, even if he did have to take a ducking with his clothes on in front of scores of people. But his family resented it, they turned against his new life, and when he finally left home for the big wide world he carried with him a bleeding mouth and a bruised face as well as a suitcase.

Ernie became a nurse in the Army and married a pretty teenager of about his own age called Joan. Everything seemed to be going along fine, but of course a battle was waiting round the next corner. It came in the form of an officer. The superior sent for him and offered him the princely sum of thirty pounds a week to take part in a large stealing syndicate. The cash was a great temptation and eighteen-pound-a-week Ernie found himself thinking it over. But he said 'No.'

Ernie thought he'd hear no more of it and when he was called for again a little while later he thought it was another Army matter. To his dismay he was accused of attacking another soldier. There were six witnesses to the trumped up charge. By some strange coincidence the soldier he was supposed to have beaten up was a good friend of the officer.

Ernie had been framed. Set-up real bad. The charge read he'd attacked the man while the balance of his mind was deranged. All he could do was pray for a way of escape to open up that would get him off the charge and out of the Army gates as quickly as possible. He found that in his times of prayer and Bible reading God really did give him strength.

The Army at first denied him a solicitor but then, after a protest from Ernie, submitted to his wishes. When the lawyer arrived he demanded to see the relevant papers but was told his client had already been found guilty. At this stage there hadn't even been a trial and the furious solicitor insisted the young soldier was British and as such could not be detained in prison without a trial. After some dilly-dallying Ernie's prayers were answered. They let him leave the Army without a stain on his character. God had won another fight for him, but yes, you've guessed it, Ernie once more forgot his promise to God. Again he went off under his own steam.

Ernie's main aim in life was to have a house of his own – and he got it. Then his chief purpose became filling it up with possessions, things his family couldn't afford when he was a kid, appliances that weren't even invented when he was a boy. Ernie's grocery business was doing well and with the money he carefully saved he was able to afford to instal central heating. That at least meant no more ice on the bedroom windows in the mornings. He saved up a bit more and bought double glazing and that meant no more condensation on the glass.

Other people didn't have these luxuries. Ernie and Joan were really keeping up with the Joneses! In fact, come to think of it, he and his wife *were* the Joneses! There was no stopping Ernie. He had everything new in existence. None of it nicked, all paid for. And his love of it ploughed an even deeper furrow in the great open field now between him and God.

Ernie thought he had everything until a doctor told him that the reason Joan was having no children was not because there was something wrong with her. She could have kids. Only Ernie couldn't give them to her. He was shattered at the news. You can't buy children.

One day he arrived home from work and told Joan he was losing his memory. The doctor put it down to the tablets prescribed for him. Gradually things got worse and Ernie started to lose the use of his hands and feet. The doctor prescribed another bottle of pills to take away the side effects. They say there's no smoke without fire. These drugs affected poor Ernie's eyesight for four years until he could manage the job that paid so well no longer, and had to leave for an Industrial Rehabilitation Unit at Egham, Surrey. While he was there Ernie became totally blind. He was also nearly completely paralysed – at the ripe old age of thirty-one. The doctors were anxious to contact Joan to make arrangements for her husband to go into a nursing home.

To add to Ernie's bitter misery in his new dark world, the voices of the physicians were telling him straight that'd he'd not be getting better. He begged, pleaded with the doctors to take him off the tablets, but there was no comfort in what the chief doctor had to tell him: 'Look old chap; there's been a bit of a mix up in the amount of drugs they've been giving you in the past. I'm afraid if we stop them now your heart could stop.'

'So what's the alternative, doc?' Ernie asked.

The doctor rested his hand on Ernie's shoulder: 'The truth is old chap that we'll have to keep you on them for the moment, and for as long as they continue your life expectancy will get less and less.'

Ernie vowed that the previous dose of pills he'd taken would be his last. When the nurse arrived with his next lot he refused them. After a brief argument she went away again to fetch the sister.

Ernie lay there, crippled, blind, and knowing there wasn't long to go unless a miracle happened. All his wealthy goods he'd spent a lifetime saving so hard for were no use to him now. He couldn't even see them if he was home. If only he had taken notice of that verse in the Bible warning people to store up treasures for heaven rather than for earth. Ernie thought about it and decided to do what he'd done so often before when he was involved in a fight. Call in the reinforcements! Pray for God to rescue him from the situation. He asked God to come and help, and use the whole sickening business for his glory and honour. He didn't actually ask to be cured.

With Ernie still refusing drugs, a healing process was already under way. It started that night and lasted three days. Towards the end of this period when the doctor made his regular visit to Ernie's bedside, he found the blankets thrown back and the bed vacant. The amazed medical staff heard a shout from outside the window and looking out saw our Ernie playing football with some other patients on the grass! He was able to play his guitar again, and drive his car. Shortly he was allowed to drive it home. The doctors said Ernie's healing was a fluke, it couldn't happen. But it had.

Ernie had to be registered as blind and paralysed for some while until he was completely recovered and the doctors could find no trace of the illness.

Just before he returned home, Ernie's wife opened the door to a young couple with a baby who had no where to stay. Joan recognised the woman as a friend of the girl lodger who was living with her at that time. They told her all their money had been stolen and so she had no reservations about putting them up for the night. When she came back from work the next evening she found they had gone – and so had Ernie's and her possessions. Anything that could be carried away had been, including Ernie's credit card. They forged his signature and ran up a bill for four hundred pounds.

Considering Ernie's condition it wasn't the best welcome home present! He and Joan decided to sell up and buy a shop in Middlesex. One day when he was behind the counter he caught a woman cheating him of some money but decided to keep quiet about it – not to forgive her, but in order to get his own back. The following morning when she came in to buy her groceries Ernie diddled her. She didn't notice. 'Serves her right,' he thought . . . 'I wonder if I could pull it off a second time!' So he tried it out again on the next customer and soon he was change-cheating all the time. Gradually the sums of money increased until Ernie got away with a really large amount, I won't tell you how, but it was in the three figure bracket.

Well, Ernie panicked when he realised what he'd done and fortunately managed to get the cash back to its rightful owner before the customer discovered the loss. Fortunate? Or are you thinking he was a bit of a mug? After all Fred, you might think, he'd got away with it hadn't he? For a short time he had. How long it would've lasted I don't know. What I do know is there are people in prison tonight solely because they didn't manage to get the money back in time.

There's no doubt about it, Ernie had sunk pretty low. He'd hung on to God in the marshy patches of his life and had then let go when the ground got firm under his feet. God, however, had not forgotten Ernie.

A young woman came into the shop. She looked around the shelves of groceries for a few minutes until it was her turn to be served. Then she spoke earnestly to him: 'You've got to leave this shop and follow Jesus!' A broad grin broke over Ernie's face. He couldn't stop laughing for a while. Gradually the seconds between each chuckle slowly increased.

Then it stopped being funny and five minutes later Ernie admitted he wanted to follow Jesus. He was led back to Jesus shortly afterwards by the customer's husband. As a result, Ernie's old mother asked God into her life too. A peace and tranquility came into her life, the kind you don't get from drink or drugs. She died of cancer, a happy woman, three months later.

You know Ernie and his battles well enough now to expect more trouble, I'm sure, and come it did. Because of what he'd read in the book of James in the Bible, Ernie felt he should work to pay back money he'd stolen from different people over the years.

It was not plain sailing because his business collapsed. Ernie was forced to close down completely and lost a lot more money in the process. But he pulled through. Now he is working at an office job for much better pay and at a career he feels God gave him. Joan is a Christian too and works five minutes away. Together they are committed soldiers for God, relying on the Lord not only in the times of battle but in between times, during the lulls in the fighting.

The last time I heard from Ernie he told me: 'I find in Jesus no insurance policy but a real peace and joy. And I make following him my life. Nothing else will do.' That, he believes, is the only way you make sure of the victory. It's tragic that people, even churchgoers, often want Jesus purely as an insurance policy and nothing else. They use him like a 999 call for help when things go wrong. Those who muck about with God like that pretty soon get messed up themselves.

Their pleas may be answered, even though they pay no premiums. But they make no 'claims' when things are going well. As a result, Satan does his best to see they escape trouble. And that, he hopes, means they can forget Jesus completely.

6: Warfare

Warfare is all around us in the world, and even the relative calm of Britain doesn't escape it. I'm not talking now about the fighting between men but the spiritual battles over all of our lives. There's a real old heave-ho going on between God and the evil forces of Satan – and when I'm doing the Lord's work I seem to be right in the thick of it!

The devil hates me preaching and gets at me many times. If he doesn't get at my body he tries to get my car to conk out on the way to meetings. Sometimes he tries to seize up both.

My car's breakdowns are a joke now wherever I go. I can take my car into a garage, have it fully serviced and checked and ready for a long journey. The mechanics will tell me it's OK. So I get in it, start it up, and half way to my destination I'll break down. Either the exhaust will fall off or the engine seizes up; something like that always seems to go wrong. I really should alert the AA when I plan to hit the road!

When the car plays up I try and have faith in the Lord – and he honours it. I've always got to the meeting. I've made people sweat many times, but I've always got there in the end. And God often shows he's in control of these annoying situations.

My last car was a Daf, and I remember taking it up

to Leeds one winter's evening when I was due to give a talk to the university Christian Union. It was a rough day and the snow started coming down when I was still on the motorway. Soon I was in a blizzard and, Bonk! my engine stopped. There I was stuck in the middle lane, terrified of causing an accident and freezing. I had a quick prayer and soon a couple of container lorries stopped and helped me push the car onto the hard shoulder. I really thanked God for those Good Samaritans.

I still had to let those expecting me know where I was. Fortunately the next service station wasn't too far up the motorway and I was able to phone and say what had happened. As I was freezing I decided to have a cuppa and started chatting to the blokes on my table. They then came out to have a look at the car; I turned the ignition on and it started like a bird! What had happened was the snow had built up under the bonnet and got onto the plugs. So I was able to go on to the meeting and although I arrived late I was still able to talk to a lot of people about the Lord and tell them what he's done for me and can do for them. The devil had tried to stop me, but God got the victory in the end.

Not long after that I got rid of the Daf and bought a Ford. A lovely car. Except when I wanted it for the Lord's business!

Going up to Liverpool a few months afterwards it packed up and I made the remainder of the journey by AA Relay, who are getting to know me very well. When I got to my friend, Ken Clapham, who should come along but a mechanic from his fellowship who had just got back from holiday and he agreed to look at the car the next day. The engine had seized up and I needed a new one. He obtained it for me, put it in, and I was presented with a bill for one hundred and ninety pounds.

At a meeting I was taking in a farmer's big barn for the Lancashire CPA, Ken told them about my mishap and they had a whip round. There was only about seventy people there but they raised one hundred and thirty pounds. It was incredible. And that wasn't the end of their generosity. When I'd broken down I'd taken off my watch and must have left it on the engine while I poked about under the bonnet. I forgot about it. I told Ken and his wife of my loss and they went and bought me a gold watch. I'd never had a gold watch in my life, not even in my thieving days! They couldn't really afford it and I couldn't really refuse it. I wear that gift now and it reminds me of God's goodness to me. But when the motor breaks down and I have to take it off I make sure I put it somewhere safe!

A few days later at Selsea, I was telling a congregation how wonderful God is and I was relating this story, not to make them feel they should donate too, but to illustrate how when God guides he provides. When I was shaking people by the hand at the door after the meeting a man put an envelope into my palm. I thought it was my expenses because some churches do that. They bung an envelope into your hand and you don't know what is inside it. So I just put it in my pocket and thanked him. Before I went, though, the secretary came up and gave me my expenses. The first thing I did when I got inside my troublesome car was open up the envelope. Inside was a sixty-pound cheque and a little note saying: 'This makes it up to your bill.' I'd got a new engine from the Lord.

On another occasion the car went up the creek yet again. I was on the way to Bristol when the red oil light came on. I took the car to a garage but they didn't know what was wrong so I called the AA. Within two minutes they had diagnosed the trouble – the oil plug lead had come off. The devil didn't stop me and I got to Bristol with ten minutes to spare before the meeting started. We had a great time but as I was nearing the end of my rabbiting, getting ready for the Holy Spirit to nudge the congregation into making a decision for God, I began to get awful cramp in my toes. It was so painful I just couldn't go on and I had to break off in mid sentence and tell them: 'Well, I've got to wrap up now, if anyone wants to hear anymore you will have to stay behind and come to the afternoon meeting.' The devil must've thought he'd won. But everybody did come back to receive another dose of God's word – and many gave their lives to Jesus that afternoon. God had turned another bit of bovva into a blessing.

The devil has a go like this all the time. These are real true instances, no question about it. Cynics may scoff at it but I believe the devil is currently the Prince of this world, and that's what Jesus Christ tells us too.

I get all sorts of aches and pain when I preach, especially headaches that I don't have at other times.

People would say it was a nervous reaction, but the thing is I'm not nervous. I feel honoured and privileged, and I feel the sense of responsibility God lays on my shoulders in trying to win people for him. But I don't believe these physical ailments are nerves. I give a short prayer requesting God to take the lump in my throat, or the headache, or whatever, away.

Sometimes I have to tell the people: 'There's a big lump in my throat today. You know when you are going to swallow something and find you can't because it hurts? Well, that's how it is with me.' I generally have a glass of water by me and I use a little pun. I hold the glass in one hand and the Bible in the other. I look at their faces, all stern they may be, and God is able to use my illness to his advantage, to make them smile and attentive to what I'm telling them. I say: 'In the beginning of this Bible here you'll find a fella's name called Pharaoh. And he hardened his heart towards the Lord and the Lord had to send him some plagues. One of them was frogs. Well, the devil also sends plagues you know, to prevent preachers from teaching, and people from listening. Preachers get attacks of diarrhoea, headaches, their cars break down, all sorts happen. I've got a lump in me throat so I've had to send up a little prayer that God will take it away.'

All their faces are on me by now, incredulous. And I say: 'Now then, the devil's given me a frog in the throat. So I takes this problem to the Lord. And the Lord says, "Fred! You drown them!" ' And with that I take a big swallow from the water and that starts everybody laughing. It's good for openers and it certainly gets rid of the frogs.

If everything has been plain sailing and the devil has left me alone, I start to get apprehensive, just waiting for it.

The Lord helps me in many other ways. Every time I shut up shop for instance to go out on work for God he always makes up my money. I get extra customers or people buy extra. When I shut up shop in the Easter holidays I know I might lose a couple of hundred pounds, and I could open on the Saturday after Good Friday. But I stay closed.

When I went to the market one springtime to pick up my veg, some of the salesmen said: 'Hey Fred, is that right you're shutting up your shop for Easter?'

'Yes,' I said.

'Aren't you worried about the money?'

'No. That's the Lord's anyway and he'll make it up alright.'

'He'll make it up will he?' asked one of them. 'OK then, I'll help him. I've got some tatters here you can have at cost price.'

People who don't know Jesus find that hard to understand but Christians know what I mean because they find he helps them like that too. I believe God is ready to help us in so many ways if only we are ready to walk in his will. We may get involved in spiritual warfare but the Lord will win through, using the strangest situation and the most unlikely people for his glory. In the Bible the Lord used an ass on a number of occasions. I've seen him use an animal too – my dog.

Doris and I have lived in our Southampton neighbourhood for over twenty years. For nearly all of that time the people have rejected us. They just haven't wanted to know us. From the time we moved in we determined to live as God wished us to, and so we took in drug addicts, prisoners, people who needed help, including policemen.

The people running a five star grocers shop over the road refused to serve us from the day we came. God closed it down for them, and although a number of people have tried to open it, they've never managed it for long. The place is now a white elephant.

Some of the neighbours complained about my car in the road so I took down the garden fence and made a little entrance. Even that caused trouble. They blocked me in with their vehicles and wouldn't let me out. All sorts of nasty things happened. They knew I was an ex-convict and nobody would speak to us for years. They would walk by on the other side of the road. People going past with Bibles under their arms, on the way to their church round the corner, were just as bad. Things came to a climax when they took my dog Limo, a very affectionate border collie. I reported the matter to the police but they never could find him.

With Limo out of the way, there was no guard on our house. It was relatively easy to steal something without setting off the alarm. When I woke up in the morning three days after Limo had disappeared I looked out of the window and found our van had gone. The police never found the thief who took that either.

I've been the victim of crime a number of times now and can appreciate how some of my own victims must have felt. I wonder if the person who stole the van ever found out its lethal fault – the gear lever used to come off in my hand sometimes! Although the insurance paid up enough for a new vehicle, there was no replacing our precious dog.

A month passed and I found myself at a big church gathering in Epsom, telling people about the persecution Doris and I were going through. A lady in the congregation was soon leaving Britain to go to Switzerland. And would you believe it, she had a little dog she would have had to leave behind. She didn't want to put it in the kennels, what she wanted most of all for it was to find a Christian home. On the way back that night I had a new friend, Trixie, a little Cairn terrier.

Doris never exercised any of our other dogs, which were all much bigger breeds, but from the first time she saw Trixie she loved her and would take her for walks. And this is how God moves in a mysterious way. The people round about us took to the dog too. God has used that little dog to bring us together. Neighbours are beginning to talk for the first time. Different people are speaking to us as I take the dog round, perhaps he doesn't look so vicious as some of the other varieties we've had! Even a bloke who used to go by on the other side with a Bible in his hand pulled up as I was coming out of the front door to take Trixie for a walk one afternoon. He stopped his car, wound down the window, and asked: 'Fred, how are you?'

I said: 'Fine, thanks very much!'

And another man nearby who hadn't spoken to me for years has also become friendly. I pulled up my van one evening and he was waiting for me. He shouted out 'Fred!'

I thought, 'Hullo, what's the complaint going to be this time?' He called me indoors, poured out all his troubles, and the Lord was able to pull him out of his depression.

As I said before, where God guides, he provides. And I've had it proved to me time and time again, despite attempts by the devil to knock me off the track.

7: Warnings

Jesus warned his followers to be on their guard against false teachers and prophets. He predicted there would be some people who would pose as him. He said these Christian con artists might even be able to do wonderful miracles to back up their claims and so deceive believers in the Lord. But we are told not even to bother to go and look for Jesus if someone tells us the Messiah has returned. We are not to believe them. For his coming will be as obvious as the lightning flashing the sky from east to west.

If somebody tells you they've had a vision of some kind, my advice would be to treat them with suspicion, just like a copper does when he sees someone out and about when all is quiet in the early hours of the morning. He stops them, questions them, and maybe checks what they say if he's not satisfied with the answers. In this way, law abiding people are able to go about their business while those spinning some yarn are apprehended. No harm is done if you're innocent.

In the spiritual sense, too, we can check up on someone from what it says in the Bible. If what they claim isn't supported in Scripture then how can they be speaking the truth? Have you ever come across anyone telling you they are Christ? Or someone who was convinced he'd been told by God he was to be a prophet? I have, and it makes me shudder to think of the damage they've wreaked on other people's lives.

I'm not talking here of the many strange religious sects springing up around the world, who on the face of it appear to be bona fide Christian groups. When you examine what they believe you find their teaching is a lot different from the Bible's. No, I mean individuals, working within the framework of the traditional church set-up and also outside it. In my travels I've met quite a few people like this, many of them well meaning, but spiritually up the spout you might say. How the devil must clap his hands and jump up and down in glee when he watches people following their falsehoods! Sometimes the deceit is obvious.

One man I know of in a mental home is convinced he's Jesus and he tells everyone just that. 'No wonder he's in a mental home,' I hear you say. 'He can't be sane to claim such a thing.' But the trouble is, he is still able to spread his message in the home. And people are being led astray as a result. This man says he's Jesus and asks the other inmates to follow him, like Christ did. Twelve of them have and he has appointed them as his disciples. They will do anything he tells them to do. There's also another fella there who is certain he is John the Baptist.

Then there are those whose deceit is more subtle. Years ago, a now middle aged wealthy farmer friend of mine, Paul, claimed he was given a vision from God telling him he would be a modern day Moses. He would lead a revival and take Britain out of its spiritual wilderness. As he grew into maturity so the vision kept nagging at him. The farm was prosperous but one day he got the urge to pack it all up. He sold everything and waited for the Christian revival to come. Part of the farm was sold on condition that for a couple of weeks each year he could borrow the land to run a Christian holiday camp. This was to be where the revival would begin, although people coming to stay had no idea of his true intentions.

Paul wanted me to join him but I saw through it and said 'No.' Nevertheless, quite a few came to believe him and trusted what he said. On the face of it he was a clean living fella, said wonderful prayers, and knew the Bible inside out.

After a while of living constantly with his claims of being Moses and hearing how he was going to lead the world to rights, Paul's wife had him put away in a mental hospital and she later divorced him.

Seven years later he was allowed out, but the rest and treatment had done nothing to dampen his vigorous preaching that revival was coming and he would lead it as God had promised him. The fact that he still maintained he'd had the vision confirmed to some people that he really was telling the truth otherwise, they thought, his hospital confinement would have removed the idea from his mind. To them, it was entirely believeable when he insisted that the Lord had put him through a period of virtual imprisonment in order to prepare him for what lay ahead. He told them Joseph had a time of imprisonment before he was allowed to lead a revival in the land, and he'd had to go through the same thing.

I told him: 'What you are doing is spreading nothing but deceit. You are deceiving yourself and you're pulling others down with you.' Knowing the Bible so well though, he was able to argue back quoting verses from Scripture and we reached deadlock. It was as hard for me to get through to him as it was for Paul to convince me of the truth of what he was doing.

'No, I'm not going to be shaken Fred,' he would say. 'God's revealed to me what's going to happen. I'm to lead the revival and the devil is trying to use you to make me drop it because the last thing he wants is more Christians. I'm sorry Fred, but you're the one who's wrong. You'll see.'

Paul was back into the money by this time, and I'm sure a fair number of those who were following him did so initially because they knew he could 'hand out'. And hand out he did. He seemed to be chucking the stuff away, spending it like wildfire.

The next I heard he had a new five thousand pound car and was preparing to buy a Mercedes. That's what he had when they put him away and his ex-wife had sold it. But he wanted a new Mercedes for when Jesus came. Maybe he thought he'd go up to heaven in it, I don't know.

Paul wanted his wife back because he said he was not really divorced. 'Never mind the law,' he told me, 'I'll change the law. Moses made the laws, now I'm going to make them. God's going to make me the law giver. Our Parliament and our Queen are going to be under subjection to me. I'll change the law so we are not really divorced and then I'll be able to have my wife back.'

'But Paul,' I pleaded, 'she's got another husband now and she no longer belongs to you!'

'Well, I've written her a letter telling her she's committing adultery,' he replied.

'And how do you expect her to return a lovely letter to you when you're telling her that?'

'Scripture tells me she does belong to me. She's my wife. I didn't divorce *her*. We took our vows. And the Bible says we're married.'

I gave up my line of questioning and turned to a different subject: 'And what about your vision? Do you still believe in it?'

'Yes,' he said. 'The revival is happening soon. It'll be at the end of the year.'

I hoped he was right, but I couldn't see it. I said: 'But a man must work and at the moment you're not. God won't choose a person who refuses to do a job. That's not a good witness.'

'Ah, but my job is to come Fred,' he answered. 'You'll see.' The year passed. It got to December. Christmas. Paul waited. New Year's Eve. New Year's Day. Nothing happened. And Paul's still waiting.

He's a dear fella, but Satan, I'm sure, has blinded his eyes. There's a lot like him. The last I heard he was back in hospital preaching to the deranged.

So there you have it, two kinds of mis-leaders. The first crazy and dragging down other crazy people with him. The second a good deal odd about him but in my opinion definitely not mad. Sane people have believed him and been thrown off the track as a result.

Then, thirdly, there are the totally normal types. Not a thing strange about them at all. They take their roles as Christians in the church, they're kind, understanding, they love Jesus, believe he died to save man from his sins . . . it's incredible to think they could possibly be undermining God's plans with what they say. But they are, they're leading many thousands of people away from the truth, often without any intention of doing so. They are the people Christians have come to rely on for their spiritual food. Don't fall out of your chair but I'm talking here of the clergy. Not all of them by a long chalk, just some. Clergymen in all denominations, be they priest, vicar or minister. And they get away with it because their congregations sit and listen and accept what they say instead of checking it out in the Bible. I'm not against the TV but I bet the devil's happy with its progress to date. It's turned so many humans into sponges.

Homosexuality is one area where I believe people are getting conned. Not that it's new, we used to have homosexuals in prison and some of them would wear jail-made make-up concocted out of paints they'd scrape off the walls. Today though, being gay has changed from being unacceptable and abnormal in the public's eye to something that is frequently acceptable and normal. 'Do what you wanna do if it doesn't hurt anybody else' has become the maxim in many circles, including some churches. So it was only a matter of time before clergymen preached that homosexuality was not really wrong, there was nothing to feel guilty about, God commanded we love one another.

Today there's even a society for homosexual vicars. This is a great comfort to people who are worried they are gay or might be. It certainly seems a comfort to these clergymen. But I'm afraid they're living in a fool's paradise. My Bible tells me in no uncertain terms that homosexuality is wrong. Woman was made for man, not man for man, otherwise none of us would be reading this, would we? I wonder what Bibles these clergymen read.

Other clergymen mislead in a host of ways. One Christmas I went to a church in Wiltshire. The bishop had granted me permission to preach there and it was reckoned to be something of a miracle because qualified preachers with a Rev in front of their name and letters after it had been turned down. Driving there, I switched on the radio to listen to the Sunday morning service and heard the vicar preaching say quite categorically: 'There's no hell. God is a God of love. There won't be judgement. For God is a God of mercy.'

I was seething with fury. How many thousands were hearing this rubbish in their homes and being conned left, right and centre by it? The devil was having a field day aiding and abetting the distribution of completely false information. It made me see red. The preacher wasn't finished yet. 'We're all sinners,' he purred. 'None of us are perfect, and God knows that. And he will have mercy upon his children because he is a God of love.' I switched the radio off in disgust.

As I rolled up in the church car park and realised a big turn out was on the cards I told myself: 'Fred, here's your chance to do something about it. Now God can use you to undo some of the damage handed out over the air. Tell them what the Bible says.'

So I did. I said: 'It's alright. I know where I am. It's C of E here in'it? And I 'aint come here to knock you but I wanna tell you something I think you should know.' They looked eager to hear what it was but when I told them I could see a few expectant faces falling.

'The vicar on the radio service earlier today said a pack of lies, some of you might've heard it. He said there 'ain't no hell. Just cos he 'ain't been there yet don't mean to say he's right. No doubt some of you believe the same thing. Well, it 'ain't true. According to the Bible he was wrong. So who are you gonna believe, eh? Man's word or God's?'

I went on to refer them to the book of John in the Bible where he writes in chapter fourteen the words of Jesus: 'Do not be worried and upset. Believe in God and believe also in me. There are many rooms in my Father's house and I am going to prepare a place for you.' But that didn't mean everyone would go there, I said. In the third chapter of the same book Jesus had a chat with a very highly intelligent fella called Nicodemus, who wanted to know what eternal life was all about. And Jesus told him no one can see the Kingdom of God unless he is born again.

'It's not your clean living, doing good, being born

into a Christian home,' I said. 'It's not coming to church and saying your prayers. No, you've all got to be born again, and that means you must believe in Jesus. If you don't, you can't have eternal life.

'The Bible has this to say: "For God loved the world so much that he gave his only Son, so that everyone who believes in him may not die but have eternal life. For God did not send his Son into the world to be its judge, but to be its saviour. Whoever believes in the Son is not judged; but whoever does not believe has already been judged, because he has not believed in God's only Son."

'Many beautiful people in the eyes of the law have done nothing wrong. But Jesus Christ says in the judgement day he is going to say "Depart from me – I never knew you." And they are going to be surprised. Why? Because they haven't been born again.

'You must believe, you've got to die to yourself and acknowledge Christ. These are difficult things to grasp, I know, but this is what the Bible tells you.'

I must've upset the vast majority of them, too, because a good 80 per cent of the congregation didn't bother to come back for the evening service. It's not fashionable to preach fire and brimstone. Christians are supposed to be nice people; they mustn't say anything that causes a rumpus; they mustn't lead the battles. But Jesus told it as it was, he didn't mince his words, and that frequently meant a shindig with the 'nice' people of the day. I took heart as I told this church what I felt the Lord was guiding me to say, knowing that I'm not called to be loved by everybody, or even to be successful, but to be faithful to God's word. Anyone can be a popular preacher if they tell people what they want to hear.

Well, these folk hadn't heard anything like this for a while as it turned out their own vicar thought the same as the chap on the radio. He didn't believe in judgement or hell either!

So many people I meet go to church not to worship God but because they love the canticles, music, incense, all the candles, pomp and ceremony. Lovely pictures on the walls, cherubims on the ceiling, and all that stuff. A lot of the people in this church were there for these sort of reasons. To bring hell into it just wasn't cricket.

It's tragic that so many lovely people get hoodwinked from the pulpit. Although they say they're Christians they get offended when you talk to them about hell and refer them to the Bible. They pick and choose what they want to believe from the Bible, which makes a mockery of saying it's God's word.

The devil blinds their eyes, you see. Even the intellectuals. It's great to be in such a privileged position of passing on the words of Jesus. The word of God is sharper than any two edged sword, it pierces their hearts, immaterial of who it's coming from.

I can open my trap and say these words from the Bible sometimes almost without realising the power of the message cutting into their hearts. I've been to a lot of churches like that one and over the months have seen scores of people give their hearts to the Lord. It's because Satan knows the power of God's word that he'll do what he can to jam it.

There's another way, too, that the devil does his work. He can be a sheep in wolves' clothing. One year up at the Christian convention at Filey I met Martin. He said he was a member of the Australian police and had been sent to England to see how security operated at British holiday camps. At the beginning of the holiday he was always causing trouble; making things difficult for the convention. I decided to have a chat with him along with some others, and to cut a long story short he was miraculously converted – or so it seemed. After the camp he was welcomed into the homes of several members of the CPA – he said he was going to start a branch in Australia when he got back. We were all keen to help him. On several occasions he came to stay with Doris and me and sometimes helped me in the shop. Once when he was with us he suddenly left leaving a note saying he'd had to hurry to London where a relative was sick. You can imagine how I felt when I discovered he'd scarpered with all my money boxes, my medals, my sentimental treasures and over one hundred pounds from the till in my shop. When we looked into Martin's background we discovered he was a con man through and through: he wasn't even an Australian, he was cockney! He'd been in prison several times and ended up back there again. So don't be taken in by people who can quote Scripture – the devil did that to Christ. Keep a loving eye on strangers who join the fellowship and pray that you'll smell a rat if there is one.

If you were the devil, how would you deceive

Christians? I know what I'd do. Just what he is doing at the moment – bung in a few false teachers. Then, so that people won't notice where the real damage is being done, create a few diversions. An obvious nutcase who claims he's Jesus for example. That'll make people think it's simple to detect the false teachers. They'll never suspect the sane . . . or will you?

8: No Escape

They called me the devil's advocate when I was in the Army and looking back I suppose they were right. They didn't come much more cunning and crafty than old Fred.

My previous training set me up well for when I was recalled in World War II. I was a marksman on all known types of weapons and soon got the job of teaching conscripts in their use. But that wasn't the only aspect of my teaching. They also learned from me all sorts of useful tips in the art of self-preservation, including how to steal undetected from the NAAFI.

I've often thought since how it would have been if I'd had a Christian faith in those days. Perhaps they'd have called me God's advocate. As it was the 'devil' tag stuck with me for many years – until only recently in fact. Now my old chinas finally know where I stand. They've actually witnessed me advocating God in front of them!

It seems incredible, I know, but at the reunion of the Somerset Light Infantry 1st Battalion in Glastonbury last year they asked me to do the epilogue! What a turnup for the books! I'd managed to attend a reunion meeting a few years previously and bumped into my old major, Jack Swann. 'What on earth is that devil's advocate doing here?' he'd asked. He'd been amazed to hear of my religious experience and was flabbergasted when he saw me drinking a fruit juice.

Others, too, had not surprisingly been shocked to find I was a preacher. I'd not had the opportunity to preach to the lads though so when I heard that the Bishop of Exeter, who usually took reunion epilogues, was unable to attend you can guess what went through my mind . . .

Well, they were all boozing, having a good night out, when up I got at the end of the evening and started talking about Jesus. Most of them just don't associate him with happy occasions so you can imagine what their reactions were. Many didn't bother to listen and carried on talking, joking and laughing. Some were polite and stopped rabbiting, and others went out of their way to show their scorn. Just like I would've done forty years earlier.

'What's all this? Git off oud of it! This 'ain't a church meeting mate! Git off!'

The shouting was causing disruption and out of the corner of my eye I could see the secretary waving his hand for me to wind the talk up. It looked as if there was nothing for it. So I started shouting too.

'Stop waving your arm,' I told him. 'Sit down and don't panic!' I surveyed the smoke-filled hall.

'Now all of you out there, listen to me. Every year you have the Bishop come here and you keep quiet while he talks to you. Well, he isn't here this year, I'm here instead. So how about keeping quiet, cos in fact I'm trying to do the same as the Bishop.' The noises of protest had gone quiet. I had their attention.

'I'm gonna talk about my saviour Jesus too, who one day you will have to stand before, whether you laugh at it now or not. Your knees will bow and your tongue confess that he is Lord. And many of you will burn in hell if you haven't received him as Lord and saviour.'

By now you could have heard a pin drop. I went on: 'Just prior to me coming up here what did we have eh? A two minute silence. And you know why? Because many of our comrades have passed away from the last time you met them. Some of them were here last year, drinking like you've been doing and are doing now. But they're not here today because they're dead. Now then, even this year there could well be some of you here who won't make it to the next reunion cos you're gonna pass on too. By the look of some of you you've been living on borrowed time for a while. And many of us here are gonna have a two minute silence for *you*.

'Where will you be then? If you're living now without Christ you'll burn in hell. So how about putting it right now, eh?'

It didn't half shake them! A lot of my pals thanked me and said: 'Thank goodness you had the courage to do that!' Others still had the needle and went off into the night moaning: 'We came for an annual do – anybody'd think it was a church service.'

Their scoffing hit me as being so hypocritical. Some were staying the night and then going to church in the morning for a reunion service, although Christianity meant nothing to them. So I told them what I thought: 'You'll be going to a church service tomorrow after a big booze up. It has no meaning to you whatsoever. You're going just to be seen.' They didn't like it.

I just thank God he gave me the opportunity to talk to my old comrades who knew me as a real villain. It was as if God had brought me back to them to tell the lads about what I'd found out about him, something I didn't know in my Army days.

My old colonel, Herbie Spurrell, had come to the meeting from his home in Wales, despite being in his eighties. He had tears in his eyes as he hugged me before he left. He gave me a court martial once but strangely he thought the world of me. He's a Londoner himself and he told me long after I was back in civvie life that many times, when me and my pal Moggie had stood before him giving our explanations for some offence or other, that he'd had to turn his head away to keep a straight face and avoid bursting out laughing. And we had no idea at the time. It's incredible what you can find out about people after many years. The old soldiers who heard me preach that night would be the first to agree.

Moggie and me always used to try and cheer everybody up. We were the rogues but when everybody was absolutely down and gasping we'd come up with a song, a real rough filthy one. It would get them all going and give them renewed strength. And that was just wordly strength. If we'd had Jesus to share then, what a wonderful strength he could have given us throughout many a dark day!

Now you might believe I was being too harsh when I told my Army mates they'd go to hell when they died if they didn't have Jesus. You may think I was trying to frighten them into making a decision. Well, I don't want to frighten anybody, just tell them the truth as the Bible says it. If the truth is frightening, I make no apologies. That's the way I see it.

None of us knows when we will die so I think it only right to preach what I believe to be true and tell people straight. It could be their last chance. And I'd be failing as a follower of Jesus if I watered down the Gospel. If I didn't say what I reckon is true then I'd be a conman. So I always tell people what the Bible says. They can make up their own minds. It's not fashionable these days to believe in hell. Word has got around that everyone goes to heaven. Cynics, and even preachers, mislead people and tell them God is a loving God and wouldn't really allow you to go to hell. Well, that's not what the Bible says. And as Christians get the basis of their beliefs from the Good Book, what makes the most sense? To believe man's word or God's word?

People can condemn themselves through ignorance. You don't *ask* an idiot who lights up a fag at the scene of a bad car smash to put the thing out. You tell him! In the same way I'm always very firm while preaching for the benefit of the person who's taking liberties with his life.

Take Hull. I was up at a big church there and during the service in walked a group of teenagers, about fifteen to seventeen years of age. There must have been twenty of them altogether, boys and girls.

They were all wearing flat caps, like the one I wear. They sat down noisily at the back. I hadn't come on to speak at that point but I could see them there, mucking about, being disrespectful. A few were bringing out fags and lighting up to try and shock everybody. As I sat watching I could see the church wardens and deacons turning round asking them to be quiet. During the hymns everybody would be standing, except this lot at the back. And when the congregation sat down, the gang stood up.

From the platform I decided I couldn't take part in the service if these hooligans were going to abuse it. I was really working myself up to a fever pitch and felt like slinging them out. When the time came for me to give my testimony I tackled the gang at the back first. I told them in my best Cockney: 'Yer in God's 'ouse nar so don't muck about in it. If yer don't want to 'ear what I'm gonna tell yer gid art nar! An' if yer gonna stay then shut up an' keep quiet!'

Then I told them I was going to talk to God. I had a word of prayer out loud, relating to these youngsters who seemed to be trying to put the boot in on the service. I talked of the consequences there could be if they did muck about. Whether it put a little bit of fear in them I don't know. I remember being very uptight about it. But you know, they did keep quiet, right throughout the time I spoke. And that amounted to about one hour and a quarter.

At the end, I went up to them, got them all together, sat down in a pew, and started chatting to them. I said: 'Come on then, why do you misbehave? What's it all about?'

They took to me and it was marvellous. They just poured out their hearts. Some had been brought up in Christian homes, they knew all the answers, others of them had heard the police would be there and thought they'd come in for a laugh.

Now they couldn't believe what they'd heard me say. They started questioning me: 'Was it real Fred? Did you really see Jesus? Was you really a villain? Why did you hate the police?'

So I called my Inspector friend over and said: 'Right then, here's a live Inspector. You ask him a few questions. You ask him about Jesus too.'

They started putting the policeman on trial; and I got another policeman over to talk to them and together they were able to strike up a relationship. The lads and the lasses there could see for themselves that policemen are ordinary people.

I feel a few bridges were built that day, not only between these youngsters and the police but between them and God. And this is what evangelism should be about; coming to the level of the youngsters, talking to them. They can still have fun, a good giggle, but there are places for it, and while in God's house they must show respect because he is the living God.

As a group they may give you the impression they couldn't care two hoots, or they may pretend they are not listening. But when they are alone it is a different story.

This group of youngsters weren't the first to come and try to disrupt one of my meetings by a long chalk. It's happened before. But one occasion really sticks out in my mind. It's an instance I'll never forget. And perhaps it explains more than anything else why I refuse to tolerate mucking about in church.

I was at a meeting in a Brethren hall down the West Country one Sunday evening. We knew that in the village the Hell's Angels motorbike lads were ready and waiting to disrupt it. Previously I'd been warned that some of them were going to come into the meeting to mess up the service.

I was ready for them, and all through the service you could hear their powerful bikes revving away and roaring up and down the road outside. But the sermon time passed without incident. Then as we were singing the last hymn, pledging our support for Jesus in the words 'I do believe', two of the leather jacket lads came in.

I can see it now, them standing at the entrance, and as the congregation sang 'I do believe, I do believe' the Hell's Angels fellas started up a hymn of their own. It was louder than the hymn we were singing. Their out of tune version, shouted above the voices of the congregation, came over as a massive sneer at our faith. The pair yelled: 'We don't believe! And we won't believe!' You couldn't fail to hear them. God must've heard them too. A couple of the elders went to get up and go for them but the motorcyclists had run off.

Two of them got on their motorbike. You could hear the engine roar. They pulled out straight into the path of a passing petrol tanker. It killed the pair of them instantly. The driver didn't stand a chance.

9: Moggie

'Look around – and you'll always see someone worse off than yourself.'

Anyone ever told you that? They were always telling that to my mate Moggie 'Monkey-tricks' McGee.

The trouble was he *did* look around – and he could never for the life of him see anybody as badly off as he was! Like me, Moggie was brought up in the East End, largely by his mother. There were four children and they were forced to fend for themselves from an early age. When Moggie was a nipper he was taken by his mum with his elder brother to see his father in the infirmary. Children weren't allowed in the wards so they waited outside on a bench. Dad had been confined there after being hit by the gas in the World War I trenches. On the way home Mum told them Dad had gone off to work. In fact he had died.

The family's living quarters was just one room. There was a big double bed in the corner where Moggie's mum and two sisters slept; he and his brother used to snuggle down at night, often hungry, on a bag of straw in front of the fire. Frequently during the winter they had nothing to burn so there was no fire and the lads had to cuddle up together so they would not freeze on the floor. As well as the bed and bag of straw there was a table, two chairs and two boxes. That was it. Their little home. They were lucky to have bread *and* dripping. But if it was just bread then Mum still made them all put their hands together, close their eyes, and say thankyou to God for what they did have. It did not mean anything to Moggie though. Try as he might, he just could not find anybody as poor as he was.

In the depressed 1920s at the age of ten he decided he would stick it no longer. If he could not buy food then he would have to nick it. Moggie's first 'job' was a tin of corned beef taken from a stall outside a shop in the Tottenham High Road. It was dead easy, he just grabbed it and ran off.

That tin of meat came in very handy. Mum was able to make a sort of stew with it, together with the vegetables Moggie's brother picked up from the gutter at the market. And so Moggie drifted into a life of crime. If he saw anything he fancied he nicked it. It went on for years and he usually got clean away.

The first time he was caught the authorities sent him to a detention home in Pentonville Road. To Moggie it was marvellous, he had never known anything quite like it. For the first time in his life he was given a bed to sleep in, a bed of his own, with sheets and blankets instead of a bag of straw with an old coat over him.

After leaving school 'officially' he went to work for a pencil company and became one of the first coloured fellas in the district. Black, blue, red, green, brown – he came home all sorts of colours because they gave him a job in the colour mills making crayons, and that was real dirty work.

By the age of eighteen, Moggie was fed up with the job and wanted adventure. Like a lot of blokes chasing excitement, he decided to 'join up' and ended up with the Somerset Light Infantry in Taunton. That was where I first bumped into Moggie – in a cell.

I forget now what it was I had done on that particular occasion but this is how Moggie came to be locked up. He went home on a month's leave to find his brother and sisters out of work and his mum in despair. They had no money or food.

Moggie had enjoyed his four months in the Army. He had new clean clothes to wear instead of the same old ones day in and day out, he had a proper bath whenever he wanted as opposed to a scrub down in the scullery, and as much good nosh as he could eat three times a day.

Seeing his family in such a terrible state really hit him and he realised he would have to be the breadwinner to help them survive. He felt a bit guilty about the good comradeship and life he had been leading and so he vowed to make it up. The family were his responsibility.

He gave his mum three pounds to stock the home up with grub and used the rest of his wages to pay off the outstanding rent. But he knew the food would not last forever so he looked around for a job and got the only one going. And it was a real stinker. Literally.

Moggie was given an old Ford truck and had to drive round the London hotels and restaurants picking up dustbins of leftovers from rich men's plates. Then he was responsible for boiling the disgusting muck up in boilers to make pig swill.

Now down the end of Moggie's road lived a policeman. Uncle Lenny they all called him. He was a real good copper. He knew Moggie and had watched him grow up. He also knew Moggie was due back in the Army. Often he watched Moggie come and go but he never said a word. He knew the family situation and the reason why the lad had not returned to his camp.

After nine months though, he decided to intervene. One day, as Moggie was coming home, he came down the police station steps and yelled: 'Come here a minute son!'

'What's up?' asked Moggie.

'Listen here young McGee. I've been watching you and from what I can see you are making an old man out of a young'un and it's not fair. So I'm going to send you back to the Army. You'll be returning tomorrow but you'll have to spend tonight down below.'

Uncle Lenny was due off work at six in the evening but despite being late leaving duty he went first to a little cafe and bought back a mug of steaming tea and a sandwich for his prisoner, paid for out of his own pocket.

'Could you do something else for me Uncle Lenny?' asked Moggie.

'What's that?'

'Could you nip along to where I was working and collect my pay? They owe me ten days, you see.'

'Now don't you worry about that young McGee,

I'll take care of it. I'll see your mum gets it and I'll do all the explaining. You just get back in that Army and look after yourself.'

That was not the only good turn Uncle Lenny did. He also hunted out Moggie's old uniform, had it nicely cleaned and pressed, and sent it on to the barracks. Without his uniform, Moggie would have been charged with desertion but as it was, all they could do him for was being absent without leave. He did three months in the glasshouse in Aldershot and finally got sent back to barracks for further detention in the cells. He had not sat there long when I was brought in, and so started a friendship that has lasted ever since. Being Cockneys we had a load in common.

Next morning, peaking out through the bars, we saw a lot of activity going on in the square. Soldiers were getting ready with their kit bags and we wondered what was up. Then the quartermaster came in and asked if we wanted any of our pay to be sent to our folks at home. We had fourteen bob a week and agreed that half of it should be posted to our families. We soon learned why he was in such a hurry to get financial matters out of the way. We were being drafted out to India.

Soon after we set sail the ship's cooks got out what we called the crown and anchor boards. Now me and Moggie had seen these illegal 'games' being used many times, but the fellas we were with all came from the country and had no idea what they were. A crown and anchor board was a dice 'game' in which if you didn't know what you were doing you found yourself in a 'heads you win, tales I lose' situation.

We observed the man running it and spotted straight away how he was cheating. 'That bloke's taking them on,' I told Moggie, 'and this lot don't realise. I don't like to see my mates being done. I'll show him!'

On the Saturday night we saw the fella cheating again. That did it. Moggie was near the bloke in a crowd of about twenty men when he felt his legs being pushed open. He did not let on though, and opened his legs wider to let me through. A while later he felt a tap on his knee and, still watching the slaughter of the innocent, opened up his legs again.

The fella running the show felt for his pocket but only came into contact with thin air. He looked down and his mouth fell open. The pocket containing all his takings had gone. I had cut the whole lot out with three nifty slashes of a cut throat razor. The bloke went berserk. 'Murder on the pocket!' he shouted. Half of me was still under the table and I knew I would have to create a diversion to get away. I tipped up the table and in the resulting confusion, as everyone grabbed their money thinking an officer was coming, I made my escape. That night, up on the deck, Moggie sauntered up to me with a quizical look in his eye. 'Was it you Fred?' I grinned.

''Ere, how much did you get?'

'Thirty-seven quid,' I said.

You might think we had enough to see us through the dreary journey with all that lolly. But the rate we gambled, drank, and gave it away we were broke again in a few days. We were what you might call handy with a pack of cards and now we could afford to play. Although we never made a lot we never actually lost. So passed the passage to Bombay.

We had some good laughs in India, and often when everyone was depressed me and Moggie would be the ones to lift them with a joke. Sometimes the laugh would backfire and we would get jankers for it. Like the gimmick we set up for Jellalabad Day.

This was the time for celebration as it was our regimental day. The soldiers could organise side shows and it would be like a fair. 'What'll our contribution be?' asked Moggie.

I thought a minute and replied: 'How about the show of the dancing duck, Mog?'

'Sounds fine, what do we do?'

'First, get a duck.'

Off we trotted to a little paddy where we knew there were some ducks. I managed to grab one and we bought it back to the showground site. There we charged the lads two annas a time to come and see our dancing duck. It would hop about, do the shuffle, the twist, almost anything, except it did not have the co-ordination of a Fred Astair.

Everybody was very impressed. After a while the CO came in, paid his money, and watched the bird doing a jig. He frowned, did an about turn, and went off muttering. Outside the room he grabbed the RSM: 'I want you on a spy job,' he said.

'Sir?' The RSM was aghast.

'Yes,' came back the reply. 'I want you to find out what makes that duck dance!'

Well, it took him less than a minute. The RSM investigated, came across the boundary line we had set up, and felt the iron plate on which the duck had been moving about. He looked underneath – and discovered our secret. A battery wired up to the plate. To make the duck dance we increased the current. We finished up in the clink for that lark – and all the money we took was given to the regimental funds.

But many times we got away with it, most frequently on kit inspections. Not everyone had all their kit so Moggie and I set up a kind of swap shop. As the officer walked down one side of the room checking people's kit, the blokes he had just passed would throw their stuff over to the other side so that the lads there had all their kit.

Eventually we got out the Army, but not for long Ten days before the war we were back – and what a reunion it was. That too was short lived, for we were sent to different places. News reached Moggie that I was somewhere in the east and he volunteered to come out too. His boat was in a massive convoy for protection on the journey. When they got to Cape Town, Moggie's ship turned north up the Mozambique channel to go to Mombasa, Kenya. They had only gone a short distance when they were torpedoed. The boat went down fast and Moggie was one of the fortunate few who managed to scramble to the safety of a life raft. His battle for survival had begun.

That evening, when hope was fading faster than the light, Moggie kept an ear open in case he heard a passing ship. He knew it was their only hope, and a slim one at that.

The only sound he heard was the water lapping on the sides of the little raft as it bobbed around helplessly in the sea. Then he became aware of someone talking. It was one of the men praying to God for safety. Moggie had never heard anyone praying before, not like this, although he recalled how his mum had made him say thanks before a meal. He could not understand it. He stared up into the sky as though he was searching for something. 'There must be somebody, or something, up there watching over this,' he thought. And then he said aloud: 'Why, why, why? Why is this happening to us?'

The praying soldier opened his eyes and looked up from his prayers. 'We will be saved,' he told him. 'We're going to be picked up you know.'

'Fat chance of that,' said Moggie. 'We're miles from bloody anywhere!'

They had been in the sea for two days and nights when a ship came into sight. It turned in a huge sweep and throttled towards them. Moggie and his pals could not tell at first whether it was friend or foe. Someone announced it was a Polish boat.

'Who are they?' asked Moggie. 'Are they on *our* side?'

'Not sure,' said one of the men.

'Polish . . . no they're not our lot are they?' asked another.

'Yea, the Poles, they're OK. They're on our side,' said the man who had been praying. 'See, I told you we'd be rescued!'

'Soon find out,' said Moggie drily.

The ship never stopped, although it did pick them up in ones and twos. It sped past, turned, picked more up, turned, and did so a number of times until all were safely on board. They were given a hot meal and a drink but had difficulty communicating because the sailors could not speak English. So at that stage they were still unsure about whether they were safe but captured, or safe and free.

'What we gonna do now Moggie?' asked his mate Paddy.

'Dunno about you me old son, but I see things like this right now. All I got in the world is this pair of shorts and this vest. You've got the same. Well, as far as I'm concerned my days as a private are over. Wherever we end up I want decent treatment and better pay.'

So it was that Moggie and Paddy promoted themselves to Sgt Majors. They were taken to Durban on the South African coast and put for a while in the grandstand of a racecourse. Again, Moggie could hear the same voice talking as he had heard on the raft. It was the praying fella, who Moggie found out was named Robert. Hearing him again really shook him up. He remembered the first time he heard Robert pray. The prayer was desperate. Now it was one of rejoicing. Perhaps God had sent that ship, thought Moggie. There and then he put his hands together and prayed his first real prayer: 'I don't know how to pray God but if it was you then I'd just like to thank you for pulling us out of a scrape. Look after us, won't you, in this war, and don't let me be frightened of whatever lies in front.'

Much hardship did lie ahead, though Moggie was not to know it. He himself was no angel. At one stage he joined with the Kings African Rifles fighting in Somalia and when the Italians capitulated he went round lifting off their watches and rings while their arms were high in the air in surrender. He collected enough to fill a kit bag one third full and used his prisoners' belongings instead of money for gambling.

Life became very cheap and there were countless tragic but comical instances. One evening in Kenya he got out a packet of fags to have a smoke and a voice said in broad Cockney: 'Got a Woodbine, Tosh?'

Moggie thought it was one of the Kenyans taking the mick, and he snapped: 'Shut your mouth.'

But the Kenyan protested in Swahili: 'I never said a word!'

Moggie did not believe him. Five minutes later he heard the same voice: 'Got a Woodbine, Tosh?'

It was one of the Italians. 'Where did you learn to speak Cockney like that?' Moggie asked, absolutely amazed. It turned out that the Italian was born in London and in fact knew more about Highbury than Moggie did. The 'blackshirts' had been round to his house and told him to get back to Italy. That particular prisoner was instantly promoted and sat in the front of the lorry for the remainder of the journey, smoking Moggie's fags as often as he wanted.

After East Africa, Moggie went to Burma. The Europeans had the Africans put on board the ship at

Mombasa during darkness when they could not see the water. Many of them had never seen the sea before. When they woke up next morning and saw water all around them they had a terrific shock. A heck of a lot of them were sick for the whole journey. In Burma, Moggie was with one of the worst mobs in the British Army. Life here was even cheaper.

But something spoke to Moggie. Two of his pals were brothers, Scots named Andrew and Pete Stewart. When they got back after a raid, this pair would not hollar and shout and boast about what they had done on it. They went away from the others and sat down in a quiet part of the nearby jungle and read their prayer books together.

Andrew, a sergeant, was wounded one day by a sniper's dum-dum bullet, just a short while before the nuclear bomb was dropped on Hiroshima. When the bullet hit Andrew it smashed into his chest and split into four pieces, making a horrific mess.

The troops were called out soon afterwards and on the hospital boat going home, Andrew sent word for Moggie to go down and see him. 'I want you to promise me you'll look after Pete,' he said.

'Course I will – anyway, what's the matter?'

'To tell you the truth, I don't think I'm going to make it back my old pal.'

'Don't be daft,' Moggie told him. 'Course you will.'

But Andrew was right. He died the following day and was buried at sea.

Moggie did look after Pete and they arrived safely back. During the journey, though, Pete challenged his guardian: 'Moggie, you must be one of the most wicked men in the world.'

'Why do you say that Pete?'

'Look, in all the time we've been together, never have I seen you put your hands together and thank our Lord for what he has done for you. You haven't got a scratch on your body and look what he has pulled you through! And thousands of others who don't know it too.

'I pray and thank God for what he's done for me – but you! You don't say anything. And Mog; if you don't go to the Lord you will never be forgiven. You will have to pay for your sins some way or another. But if you do go to the Lord and have the Lord with you, you will finish up completely forgiven. You will go to heaven, but if you don't then you won't.'

Moggie had never really been spoken to like that before and it upset him. But he held his tongue for the sake of the friendship. It set him thinking though, and he had hardly time to consider the lecture before Pete dropped another bombshell: 'Andy's not really dead you know.'

'Not really dead?' Moggie thought Pete had gone nuts.

'The important part of him is still alive Moggie. That's what Christians believe. It's only that old mangled body rotting in the sea.'

Moggie felt sorry for Pete. Losing his brother like that, it was playing on his mind . . .

Moggie's story continued through many more adventures, a lifetime of ups and downs. I told you in my last book, *Going Straight*, how we met up again in Tiverton, some thirty years after we lost contact.

He was involved in a road smash with a bus on the way to work one morning in the ice and did not know where he was for nearly a month. But he pulled through and although he is partially crippled now it is great to see the old sparkle in his eyes when I go down to visit him occasionally at weekends. The old 'Monkey-tricks' McGee is still there when his old body lets him. Three years after his accident he was so injured that he could still not walk. He used to stand at the street door of his terraced house and watch the world go by.

Some of the yobbos locally thought he was the village idiot, and when they charged down his street one night they tried to push him out of the way. The adrenalin shifted through Moggie's veins just like it did in the old days and brought new life to his weak body. Before they knew what had hit them he had karate chopped them flat out on the pavement!

I smiled when I heard that story, but what touches me so very much more is that Moggie took Pete's advice, given all those years ago. He went about it alone until he was a pensioner. Now God has brought new life to him. It took nearly a lifetime for it to fully sink in that God was watching over him and caring for him through thick and thin. He eventually came to the Lord, as Pete suggested, to thank God for what he had done for him and ask forgiveness for his sins.

Moggie sometimes recalls the words given to him in his youth: 'Look around – and you'll always see someone worse off than yourself.' And for the first time in his life, despite his sickness, he really can. I do not mean that Moggie has become rich in his old age, it is still tough going, but he is spiritually wealthy. Now he says, 'God's given me a helluva lot, he's altered me from when I was ready to throw in the towel. He's made life worth living.'

10: Heartaches

Lots of people think life must be pretty cushy once you're a Christian. Well, let me put the record straight. The Lord's work can be a heavy cross to carry! Many times there are heartaches. Particularly with one's own family.

Now then, many people I meet reckon all my relatives must be Christians considering what God has done for me. I wish they all were and I pray they will be but I'm afraid this is not so. And that's one of the biggest heartaches of all. Anyone who has come from a big family like me will know exactly what I mean when I say it's no easy road you travel on when you're trying to go Jesus' way and your dear ones don't really want to know. If you do find it no trouble then I'd suggest you consider if you really are following Christ.

I'm prepared to go where Jesus calls me, and that alone could precipitate a suicide. For there's a part of London where one of my relatives lives and she threatened me one Christmas Day that if I ever went there to preach she would kill herself. She told me and Doris in no uncertain terms she would rather take her own life than have me talking within a few miles of her house. The reason is she's worried about the respectable neighbours discovering that she was connected with an ex-criminal!

It's a terrible dilemma – should you do the Lord's work or stick by those close to you? When the two clash, which do you put first?

The devil will put all sorts of barriers in front of your path to stop you doing what God wants. He will try his hardest to set you against your family, wife or husband. When you are close to someone it hurts most if you disagree.

An old friend of mine Mary has been a reason for heartache too. For six months do you know where her home was? She lived in a rubbish chute at the bottom of one of those tower blocks. She used to get so drunk that she'd pass out in all the muck and filth, and while she was sleeping unexpected visitors would come and abuse her body in a horrible way, and a painful one too. The visitors were rats. Scores of them. And they used to gnaw at her legs. I suppose they weren't used to getting a good cut of meat chucked down with all the garbage in those days. She had illegitimate children, a very unhappy life, and the police kept picking her up.

After a while of rough living she came down to Southampton to live with us. Doris nursed her and brought her back to respectability. In the eight weeks she was here she really smartened up. To cap it all the Social Security people sent her a cheque for over two hundred pounds. At the time we didn't know. She must have notified her son in London, he came down to collect her, and when we got back from the shop one afternoon she'd gone and there was a little note to say she'd returned to London. Someone was ill, she'd had to go, and she'd let us know how she was. But she never did come back.

Months afterwards she was back like a dog to its vomit. She was drinking heavily again and wanted to return to us. I said: 'No, you've made your bed, now you've got to lie in it.'

Doris and I often prayed for her, like we do for other old friends and family. It was a great joy when she attended my baptism at Shepton Mallet Baptist Church, followed by my wedding. (We decided to get married again, so I could renew my vows. The first time I went up the aisle I was so blind drunk I saw everything through a haze, and the spiritual angle was a travesty.)

Today Mary is a different person, living in a block of old people's flats. I have several Christian friends going in to meet her and I always call in whenever I'm her way. Course, she still swears, it's part of her nature, but she's clean, got a nice little room, and it's the first time in her life she's had decent furniture. She listens intently as we talk to her about the Lord and we still pray that she too will make a decision to commit her life to Christ.

Christians mustn't forget to have a little chat to God about their loved ones. You can get so caught up in church matters, youth work, whatever, that you ignore your friends and family while on the other hand you're calling strangers 'brother'. I've seen it happen! Witnessing to them can be a hard old business but take heart. With God all things are possible. I had longed and prayed for my mum to find the Lord many a time. I never gave up. The result was fantastic.

On her deathbed Mum finally took Jesus as her Saviour, trusting in him to take away her sins and give her a wonderful new life in heaven. Some of her last words were of reassurance to me: 'It's alright Freddie. I do believe. My Mate will look after me.'

So I keep on praying for those close to me who don't yet know how Jesus can straighten out the problems in your life and top you up with his peace, and I hope you keep on praying for your friends and relatives. Don't give up, even when they do come to find their 'Mate'. They need the prayers then as well.

I'm telling Jesus every day about someone very special to me and Doris. His name's Trevor. We call him our other son. I met him in a strange way.

Some years ago I used to go round the schools to have chats with the clever bods in the sixth forms. One place I went to near my home was a college. A big fella got up while I was talking and walked out. I thought he must've been browned off with what I was saying. He didn't come back.

Months after this incident I was phoned one night by the probation service telling me about a lad at the college who'd teamed up with a chap twice his age to do a blackmail on one of the students there. The boy was sitting for his exams and had good prospects but going to prison would mean he'd probably miss the opportunity of taking them so the probation service wanted to know if I'd be prepared to look after him. A judge was going to come down for the hearing and it seemed as if they were going to put the frighteners on him. I understood there was the possibility that if a place could be found for the boy he might not be sent away. But the difficulty was they couldn't find anybody willing to take on the lad.

I weighed it all up and eventually said I would. On the day of the trial I was requested to go to Winchester to visit the boy. I learned he was a clever lad, although in build he was a giant of a man. Six feet six inches tall and seventeen stone, they told me!

As I went into the cells he saw me and stood up straight away and towering above me blurted out: 'I apologise sir that I walked out of your meeting; it wasn't because of anything you said but I had an appointment.'

I hadn't actually realised that Trevor was the very same fella who left the class so hurriedly when I visited his college earlier that year.

The probation officer introduced us: 'Mr Lemon, this is Trevor; Trevor this is Mr Lemon. If the court agrees to bind you over then Mr Lemon is the person who will look after you. But on the other hand if you go to prison . . . well, Mr Lemon says he would still be prepared to visit you and keep in contact.'

Trevor's own parents had disowned him. What happened to him is going on in lots of homes where there are professional men and women who are too busy for their children. He didn't even know what it was to call his father 'Dad'. Trevor had to stand to attention and call him 'Sir'. And from an early age he was disbelieved in everything he said.

He'd always had to be a sort of family slave and even as a youngster he'd been made to swot, swot, swot over his school books. There was no love whatsoever from his parents. In the public eye they were esteemed because they'd been decorated by the Queen for their services. But in reality they couldn't look after their own child properly. By the time he was fifteen, Trevor was a giant and wasn't prepared to sit and take it any longer. One day when his dad gave him a ribbing he just exploded. Everything that had been bottled up inside him over the years suddenly erupted and he gave his father a terrific hiding. He kicked his ribs in, beat him up terribly, really let it all go.

I sat through the court case in the waiting room outside until I was called to the witness box to swear I'd be prepared to look after him. It was strange being in court again. The judge gave Trevor an awful dressing down. You'd have thought he was going to prison for ten years. It was a real frightener. But then the judge added there were a number of mitigating circumstances and he was prepared to give Trevor a chance. He was bound over into my care and told that any such time as I informed the court he wasn't behaving, or hadn't done as directed, he would go to prison for a very long while.

Now this boy was arrogant to everybody and I wondered how he'd get on living with Doris and me. But right from the time he came through the living room door, stooping low to get his massive hulk through the frame, we never had any difficulties. He called Doris 'Mum' from the word go and to us he was as meek as a lamb, he'd do anything for us. We got on a treat. And he was so clever too.

Ever met those psychologist types who can virtually prove to you you're not actually here? You know, the sort of people who'd say you were not really reading this, you were imagining it! Well, Trevor was like one of them. He could tell you all about the molecules, all about the atoms, all about the formulas for drugs and goodness knows what. But speak to him about the simplest of things and he wouldn't have a clue.

'See if you can get that settee through the door then if you're so bright,' I'd say.

Trevor would struggle. He'd try it one way, then the other. Then he'd put it down and scratch his head, turn the furniture upside down, and have another go. But he wouldn't be able to work that out, and eventually he'd shrug his shoulders and admit defeat. It was nice to know old Fred wasn't completely daft!

Trevor showed us great respect, always called me Mr Lemon, and in fact he seemed to grow even bigger while he was with us. Not surprising really when you consider what he'd manage to pack into his stomach. When he ate with us, Doris would give him a huge plate of meat. We'd only get one meal a piece from a large joint of lamb on a Sunday. After Doris had carved my portion she'd put the whole leg on Trevor's plate, pile the vegetables up like a mountain over the top, and cover the lot in lashings of thick gravy. You've never seen anything like it unless you've been to the zoo at feeding time. Trevor would pick up the whole joint and tear off the meat with his teeth. In between each munch he'd pop a whole potato into his mouth. It was an incredible sight.

I wouldn't say he was a pig. He just didn't know

any manners. Even in a restaurant he was the same and it would be a bit embarrassing because there you'd be, trying to eat in a dignified manner, and he'd be next to you shovelling it down as if there was no tomorrow. Say it was a Chinese restaurant. Everyone might order one Chow Mein but he'd ask for two. And when he got through them he used to eat all our leavings. He never liked to see anything left behind. If you couldn't manage it all he'd take it off you. He was good at helping himself.

As I said, Trevor was a clever lad, and he showed initiative in other areas. If he'd been given a chance he'd have gone to university, but when he applied the school revealed his probation record and the university wouldn't take him. At that point, no university would take him unless he'd had twelve months in industry to prove himself, and the school even put the block on that. So Trevor rebelled – and did it his way. Got qualified under his own steam.

One day he told me: 'I'm going to Australia. You won't tell anyone will you, only there's nothing for me here. And if my parents want to know – don't tell them anything.'

His mother later wanted to contact him again so she used to write letters and ask me to send them to his secret address. I was put in a difficult situation because Trevor had already said: 'Don't send any letters from her to me. I don't want to know nothing.' As Trevor wouldn't allow me to send them on I used to tear them up. They never said much, just two or three lines in each letter, and never 'Dear Trevor' 'Love Mum' – just 'Trevor' at the beginning and 'Mother' at the bottom of the paper.

Trevor was successful in business, he worked in the Antarctic, the Middle East and Africa. All under his own steam, just like the man in the famous Frank Sinatra song 'My Way'.

When he came back to England he treated our home just as we wanted him to, as if it was his own. It was his base. We'd get a note saying: 'I'll be back again tomorrow' and I'd go to the airport and meet him. He was a kind hearted fella, paid all our fares when we went to see him out in the Middle East.

Now he's married with two young children and thinks he's got everything he needs. He's done it his way. But not God's way. I saw him again last year but it was the same as ever. I could never reach him with the Lord. That's what really saddens me.

He's been doing things his way for so long now it's difficult for him to be willing to let him give his life over to someone else's control. God's. And after his experiences in life with his family it's hard for him to believe there actually is a God, let alone one who cares. I tell him: 'God loved you so much he sent his own son to the world to prove he really did care. And that love cost him his life. He died for the love of us but proved he spoke the truth when he rose from the dead. Now, he's just waiting to come into your life. Just admit to him your wrongdoings and ask him to forgive you and help you make a new start. And he will. You will find peace, just like I have. He'll always be with you if you are prepared to commit your life to him, Trev.'

But he just grins. The Gospel is like water off a

duck's back to him. We believe one day Trevor will become a Christian. It'll be great when that prayer's answered! Meanwhile, despite the heartache, I can't help but give a little smile when I think of him.

I remember how he'd tell me about the atoms and the molecules, the power behind them, how though you couldn't see them you could see their effect and the evidence of their existence in the surrounding matter. And I wonder how it is that like so many people with high IQs he finds it far harder to believe in God!

As I say, I believe one day my prayer for Trev will be answered. Just like it was, as I told you earlier, for old Moggie. Perseverance in prayer pays off.

I tell people not to be disheartened when they think God is failing to answer prayers for the conversion of a loved one. The message is 'Never give up'. After all, Jesus never gives up on us.

Remember my old friend Mary? I've prayed for her for over 30 years; without any apparent results. I'll continue praying for her in future too. Now, though, God is getting a bit of a different prayer concerning her – one of thanksgiving. For a few weeks ago she finally gave her heart to the Lord Jesus. 'I don't know much about Him,' Mary told me, 'All I know is I've met Him.'

What's more is that her friends in the old people's home are in no doubt either. She's got the local minister to come in and start up a string of services for them!

11: Encounters

I have encounters of the most amazing kind wherever I go. Many of them take some believing but they are true.

I'm not easily shocked but I was when I met Angie. She was in her early twenties and was a punk. I had been primed to watch out for her because her language could be disgusting and the church where I was preaching didn't want me to be shocked.

As a baby Angie was abandoned and it appeared she grew up very much like me. After the service she started talking to me. She had heard how I had gone from one home to another at an early age, and how I rebelled against society. Angie might have had her own particular way with words but it was not the words themselves that shook me. It was *what* she said.

I couldn't imagine how she could be foul mouthed because she looked such a beautiful girl. A real cracker. As we talked, people were watching us, no doubt speculating about such an unlikely duo.

What shocked me was that she was obviously a gangster. She told me how she went around beating people up and got thrills just thinking about mugging people. Angie absolutely hated the police and asked me about my hatred of them and how I was able to get rid of it. She was sick of the way she behaved and wanted to rid herself of the hate inside. I told her how God could fix it for her. Below the hate she was crying out for love, but I warned her she would not find it by sleeping around as she was. I said: 'You're very attractive. Why don't you use it for the glory of God? He's given you a wonderful figure, but not for you to abuse it.'

Other people abuse their bodies in different ways such as getting blotto on drink. I see so much of the distress and hardship it causes. But nothing is too tough for God to sort out.

Bill used to get in such a bad state when he was on the bottle that he would gamble all his wages away. Some weeks he wouldn't have any money left to pay his debts and nothing for his young wife Miriam and the children. There were many heartaches in the family because of it, suicide attempts were made and there were tremendous rows. Eventually she kicked him out. Only one person in his family took him in. That was his old grandmother. She was a Christian and he would take refuge in her home until he had sobered up.

This particular weekend, Bill got boozed up to the eyeballs and Miriam refused to let him in the house. No other relatives would have him so Bill made for his grandmother's. He told her he was going to do himself in because he was at the end of the road. The grandma gave him coffee and started talking to him. Then she played one of my tapes. Now, that lasts around an hour. After it was over he said: 'Nan, play it again.' So she did – and again, and again. In all she put that tape on four times, all through the night into the early hours of the morning. As it finished for the fourth time, Bill said: 'If God can do that for Fred Lemon, he'll do it for me.'

'He certainly can Bill,' said Gran. And he did. Not long afterwards Bill came along to one of my meetings and was gloriously saved. He has been off the booze now for a number of years and through him Miriam has given her heart to the Lord too. So have the children. Bill still finds it a battle, but it's one he is winning.

Talking of battles reminds me of my encounter with Nick. I was talking at a Methodist church about hatred. How we can put on a false front and seem nice to people but deep down our hearts may be full of evil intentions. I said: 'People may be able to kid everybody else but the Lord knows their intentions. He sees them scheming. There may be people here now listening to the prayers and taking part. They listen to the reading of the Bible but suddenly their minds are wandering and although they are in the house of the Lord their hearts are far from him.'

As I spoke, a fella who must have been in his early thirties got up and walked out. Ten minutes later he returned and sat down again. After the meeting I was introduced to him. Nick was a businessman and he revealed he had been crossed in a deal to the tune of a few thousand pounds. As he sat listening to what I said, he thought I was speaking directly to him. I was saying exactly what was going on in his heart. At the very moment I opened my trap to say 'right now there might be someone here who's scheming', he was doing just that. He was swearing revenge on the person who had swindled him and there in God's house was working out the details of a business contract that would give him, he thought, a great deal of satisfaction. A contract *on* his business enemy. He was going to employ a lynchman to go and break the person's legs. He was ready and willing to pay a few hundred pounds once the evil job was done.

As I talked to him, Nick told me how he'd left the church and made for the pub across the road. He was determined to have a few drinks in order to drown his conscience. The barman poured him a large whisky. But as he sipped it he heard a voice inside him saying: 'Go back, go back Nick.' He drank the whisky up, swallowed his pride, and returned. And that night he gave his heart to the Lord.

In church Nick was known as a Christian, but the truth was he was just a church goer. He went out of respectability. And he'd walked out because he couldn't stand any more of what I was saying.

Many other encounters I've had with people have left me marvelling at the power of God. There was once a chap, Ian, who bought a second hand tape recorder. The seller threw in a couple of tapes and said: 'One of them is a religious thing, all about Fred Lemon, but you can scrub it.' As it happened Ian took it home, put it on, and was converted through it.

Some of the funniest things that happen occur in my shop. Lots of people must be feeling the financial squeeze and are coming in to buy just one onion, half a pound of carrots, or half a big potato! I find it embarrassing to charge them anything.

Then there are other customers who give me some yarn about wanting the best looking fruit because they are visiting old people in hospital. But they don't know I know that the fruit is really for themselves. They don't want bananas with little brown marks on because they plan to put it on show in their expensive fruit bowls and it's got to be nice in case a visitor comes.

You will always get the customer who is waiting in the queue and starts complaining to the person on either side about the standards of the vegetables she bought the week before. When I question them out loud so that everyone in the shop can hear they admit they didn't even buy it in my shop.

But what gets to me most of all is when people start blaspheming in my shop. It really hurts me to hear them say: 'Jesus Christ!' I tell them many times not to take the name of the Lord in vain. It pulls them up really sharp. Society tolerates Jesus' name being used in a swearing sense now. But it is not just any other name. There is real power in the name of Jesus and people who abuse his name recognise it too. It gets rid of their tension. They don't shout out 'Allah' or 'Buddha'.

Jesus brings relief, a release, as many of the people in this book have discovered. I believe it would be wrong for me to say nothing when Jesus gets abused. Jesus will always come to those who call on him and really mean it. But I can't help wondering how you would react if someone kept shouting out your name and didn't really want you. After a while you'd stop answering, perhaps not realising the call was serious. I believe there is somebody calling you right now. He called my name and I answered. 'Tell them Fred, that what I've done for you I can and will do for them if they are willing,' he said. 'Some will think you're a nutter. But it's their choice. You tell them I'm calling.'

To me, Jesus is the most amazing encounter of all.

Also by Fred Lemon in Lakeland

BREAKOUT

Fred Lemon with Gladys Knowlton

It was very quiet in my cell after the warder had escorted me back from the 'dungeons' – the punishment cells. I threw myself on the hard bed, a black bitterness of soul filling me. Tomorrow, I vowed, I would get hold of the sharpest knife in the mailbag room – and there would be murder done. Weary and tormented I pulled the coarse blanket round my shoulders and closed my eyes.

Something made me sit up suddenly. There were three men in the cell with me; they were dressed in ordinary civvy suits. The man on the right spoke:

'Fred,' he said, 'This is Jesus . . .'

Fred Lemon, a confirmed criminal, on the eve of attempting to break out of Dartmoor, unexpectedly broke out spiritually, and found this freedom far greater than that of the open moor.

This story of an East End child who grows into a violent criminal simply and powerfully shows how criminality breeds and takes a man step by step into the abandonment of hell, and yet how Christ can meet a man even there.

GOING STRAIGHT

Fred Lemon with Gladys Knowlton

In this book Fred invites you to come and share some of his experiences since the prison gates clanged behind him. He says, 'You will find in these pages that even the most ordinary setting – a shop, a homely room – can become the place where miracles take place, and that extraordinary things can happen to the most ordinary people.'

UNDER GOD'S WORD

Jim Packer

Is the Bible all true? And is it important that it should be? Dr. Packer, the best selling author of *Knowing God*, takes a decisive stand on these questions. But he goes beyond the issue of inerrancy to the more important one of authority – what is the point of winning the battle for the Bible if in the process we lose our understanding of its role? The Bible is central to both personal and public worship. To recover truly biblical faith and practice we need to restore the Bible to its rightful place in the lives of present-day Christians and churches.

Writing with a deep pastoral concern Dr. Packer brings us back to devotion and worship as the key to understanding God's word and appropriating it for ourselves. *Under God's Word* is a challenging reminder that it is nothing less than our souls which are at stake in this debate.

THE GOLDEN COW

John White

Christ drove the money changers out of the Temple with a whip. The Old Testament prophets charged Israel with idolatry, accusing her of prostitution. The people of God had sold themselves to the allurements of political security, social acceptability and economic growth. Are we doing the same? Is the church today worshipping the golden cow of materialism and success?

John White begins to answer this question by considering the property-centred outlook of many churches. Then he examines the fund-raising techniques of Christian organizations and the organizations of Christian businesses. Finally, he moves into the frequently statistic-ridden realm of evangelism. In this prophetic book John White asks us to consider whether we, too, are worshipping the golden cow.